Getting To Know You

Marie-Louise von Franz, Honorary Patron

**Studies in Jungian Psychology
by Jungian Analysts**

Daryl Sharp, General Editor

Getting to Know You

The Inside Out of
Relationship

DARYL SHARP

For all those I have ever been related to,
especially the women.

Canadian Cataloguing in Publication Data

Sharp, Daryl, 1936-
  Getting to know you

(Studies in Jungian psychology by Jungian analysts; 55)

Includes bibliographical references and index.

ISBN 0-919123-56-2

1. Interpersonal relations.
I. Title.
II. Series.

BF636.S53 1992   158'.2   C92-093494-3

INNER CITY BOOKS
Box 1271, Station Q, Toronto, Canada M4T 2P4
Telephone (416) 927-0355
FAX (416) 924-1814

Honorary Patron: Marie-Louise von Franz.
Publisher and General Editor: Daryl Sharp.
Senior Editor: Victoria Cowan.

INNER CITY BOOKS was founded in 1980 to promote the
understanding and practical application of the work of C.G. Jung.

Cover: "Four Vessels," acrylic painting by Victoria Cowan (© 1989).

Index by the author

Printed and bound in Canada by
John Deyell Company Limited.

CONTENTS

Preface

We become aware of the void as we fill it.
—Antonio Porchia, *Voices.*

"Here we are again," said Rachel.

She was lying on the sofa in a provocative pose. Rainbows lit her hair, bounced off the walls. Rachel is to me what Beatrice was to Dante. She shows me the way. Well, more or less. Sometimes she just goes her own way and I go astray.

"Yeah," I grumped.

I was feeling at loose ends. The business was humming along, it didn't need me. All the records were up to date, all the letters answered. My desk was clean as a whistle. I had nothing to do. I felt the Void closing in.

Where does my energy want to go? I wondered.

"It's a good time for a holiday," said Rachel. She flashed me a bright smile. She loves to travel.

I grimaced.

"You have to learn to just *be.*" said Rachel.

"I will, I will. Next year. Maybe."

I wandered into the back yard. Arnold was there. He was scratching in the earth and humming to himself. We'd lived together in Zürich while we were training to be analysts. Now he was a neighbor. Arnold had a garden of his own, but sometimes he worked in mine too. He looked up and saw my mood.

"Doesn't your heart sing to see growing things?" he said.

I shrugged.

"Don't you thrill to the change of seasons—spring water rushing through the woods, the heavy heat of summer, multicolored leaves in the fall, the pristine brightness of snow?"

I yawned.

"Come," said Arnold, "smell the flowers."

He led me around like a blind man. He stuck my face in the hybrid roses. He pressed my nose against the lilacs and marched me past the cedars. He pointed out the impatiens, the lilies and petunias, the giant bulb begonias that took two days to plant.

"A garden is a very special place," said Arnold. He snapped his purple suspenders.

"Yes," I agreed. But it made no difference.

He sat me down by the pool and disappeared. I stared at the rippling water and thought about going to bed. Sometimes it's the only way out. I don't think about what to do when I'm sleeping. But then there are dreams. I decided not to go to bed.

Arnold came back with a cold shaker of lemonade and a plate of my mother's shortbread cookies. I chewed an ice cube and wondered if I'd ever be happy sitting on my hands.

"Listen to this," said Arnold . . .

It was late evening when he left. I felt a lot better. I gathered up the dishes and raced into the house.

Rachel was curled up in a wing chair, reading a thriller.

"I've got it!" I cried, rubbing my hands. "I know what to do!"

Rachel frowned. She enjoys a good read and doesn't like to be disturbed, but what can you do.

I told her what I had in mind.

"I don't know," she said. "Why don't you write a novel?"

"I have no imagination. I can embroider on reality, that's all."

"Dummy," said Rachel affectionately, "that's what novelists *do.*"

I said nothing. I know some and I'm not like them at all. They fly, I'm earth-bound. They can create worlds that never were or might have been. I'm stuck in this one. Their Rachels—or Roberts—must be quite different.

Rachel mused. After a time her eyes lit up. She smiled.

"But what if Arnold spills the beans?"

"I can edit it."

Note to the Reader

The content of this book grew out of a seminar based on C.G. Jung's essay, "Marriage As a Psychological Relationship."

Those taking part in the five two-hour sessions included several professional therapists, a real estate agent, two house-wives, a postman, an advertising executive, a restaurant owner, two college professors, a Protestant clergyman and a Catholic priest—thirteen in all, six women and seven men. Their ages ranged from twenty-eight to sixty-three.

Seminar One

Before we begin, I want to make a few things clear. My agenda is not writ in stone, and I know that linear progressions are not everyone's cup of tea, but I always like to at least start off with some structure in mind. So my idea is simply to work our way through "Marriage As a Psychological Relationship" paragraph by paragraph, and see where that takes us.

Jung wrote this essay in 1925. My own feeling about it is that it touches on, or leads to a consideration of, just about every important concept of analytical psychology. It's very short, only twelve pages, so it can easily be read in one sitting, but it has as many layers as an onion. Like most of Jung's writings, something new jumps out at you each time you read it. Some of that is because where we are ourselves, our own experience and level of understanding, is always changing. In anything we read, we tend to fasten on what's important to us, what we can identify with at that moment, and we're never the same the next time. This is particularly true for material that deals with psychological issues.

I think it isn't necessary to have a knowledge of Jung's other work to appreciate what he has to say here. Obviously, some of you will be more familiar with the terms and concepts he uses than others are. We'll deal with that as we go along. Jung never wrote a systematic summary of analytical psychology—he never said everything in one place—so just about anything of his will lead you to something else he wrote, just to get your bearings. Fortunately, there is a very good index to Jung's *Collected Works*.

Remember this is a seminar, not an *ex cathedra* lecture, so please feel free to ask questions any time.

To begin at the beginning, then, with the title—"Marriage As a Psychological Relationship." What do you make of that? Why does Jung use the word "marriage" and not, say, "friendship"?

11

He's only concerned with legally sanctioned relationships?

No, I don't think so. Of course, one could approach this essay with the idea that Jung is writing only about what happens between husband and wife, but what about other definitions of marriage, for instance "any close union" or "a true marriage of minds"?[1]

We know this was originally written to be included in a German volume called *Das Ehebuch* (The Book of Marriage). It's possible that the title was a bow to the mores of Jung's time. In 1925 a close union between a man and a woman was conventionally synonomous with being legally married. Nowadays there are quite as many common-law relationships as marriages, and probably as many again that fit no legal description.

We know too that Jung had intimate relationships outside his marriage with Emma, and from all accounts these were very important to his understanding of himself.[2] I imagine they also contributed to his ideas on the archetypes, and particularly his concepts of anima and animus, how these influence a relationship. Later in this essay he talks about that.

How his relationships influenced him?

No, I wish he had! Even in his autobiography, *Memories, Dreams, Reflections,* he says very little about how his relationships affected his theories, his model of the psyche—well, except for what happened between him and Freud in the early years. Otherwise, we can only guess.

I'd love to hear from Jung himself how, for instance, his long-standing liaison with Tony Wolff affected his ideas. But he never wrote about that. On the other hand, I can respect Jung's view that whatever he might say about what happened in his outer life, it would be "hollow and insubstantial" compared to what happened inside, and that he could only understand himself "in the light of inner

---

[1] *American Heritage Dictionary.*

[2] See esp. Barbara Hannah, *Jung: His Life and Work: A Biographical Memoir* (New York: G.P. Putnam's Sons, 1976), pp. 117ff.

happenings."[3] That was the most important thing to Jung and with few exceptions that's all he wanted the world to know about.

I think Jung's remarks in this essay apply to relationships of just about any kind. Maybe they aren't relevant to what happens between casual acquaintances—professional associates and neighbors, say, or those we meet going about our business in the course of a day . . .

You mean shopkeepers, bank tellers and so on?

Yes, that's what I had in mind, but I'm not at all sure it's fair to leave them out! You see, I'm thinking particularly of relationships where complexes are liable to be activated, where strong emotions come into play. This can happen between you and your dentist, or your dog! And there's often a lot of heat involved in acquaintanceships an outsider would call casual.

Obviously there are many degrees or levels of relationship. For practical purposes we might restrict our considerations to those that are more or less intimate, like lovers, close friends, relatives, that kind of thing—but I certainly wouldn't limit the relevance of Jung's insights to what goes on between husband and wife.

What about one-night stands?

Why not? They can be very emotional. And who knows if a so-called one-night stand might not develop into a long-term partnership? A one-night stand is only that in retrospect. At the time it happens, everything is *in potentia*. There is or was an apparent attraction. It might come to nothing, it might develop. Who's to know? Least of all the two involved. They are moved by unseen forces. Tomorrow is another day. Both may be mystified by what happened. That's when a psychological perspective can be helpful.

Let's look at the first paragraph of Jung's essay.

> Regarded as a psychological relationship, marriage is a highly complex structure made up of a whole series of subjective and objective

---

[3] *Memories, Dreams, Reflections,* ed. Aniela Jaffé (London: Fontana Library, 1967), p. 19.

factors, mostly of a very heterogeneous nature. As I wish to confine myself here to the purely psychological problems of marriage, I must disregard in the main the objective factors of a legal and social nature, although these cannot fail to have a pronounced influence on the psychological relationship between the marriage partners.[4]

The focus of this essay seems to be on what happens between men and women. Do you think it also applies to same-sex relationships?

I think it does. In my analytic practice I see the same psychological issues arising in homosexual relationships as in any other, but as we go on we may hit upon things you think don't quite fit a gay relationship. Let's talk about them then.

I was only thinking about me and my girlfriend, and the guys my husband hangs out with. We're not gay.

Yes, well . . . I expect we'll come to that later also.

First off, Jung concedes that marriage—and again, we are taking this to mean virtually any close relationship—is a highly complex structure. Although he intends to limit himself to purely psychological problems, he acknowledges that objective factors have an influence on what happens psychologically. What kind of factors might he be thinking of?

Problems with money? How to raise the kids?

What the neighbors say?

I know those who were in love and even lived together quite happily until they got married. Then all hell broke loose!

Yes, we all know that happens. Money, in-laws, kids, where you live, the kind of work you do and so on, these would all be objective factors, namely, things in and of the outside world that are liable to

---

[4] *The Development of Personality,* CW 17, par. 324. Subsequent references to this essay are to paragraph number only. [CW refers throughout to *The Collected Works of C.G. Jung* (Bollingen Series XX), 20 vols., trans. R.F.C. Hull, ed. H. Read, M. Fordham, G. Adler, Wm. McGuire; Princeton: Princeton University Press, 1953-1979]

have an effect on a relationship.

Your comment about getting married is an interesting one. Until there's a socially acknowledged bond betwcen two people, they can feel free and separate. As soon as they declare themselves as a couple, they're fair game for other people's opinions. What keeps them together? What does he see in her? Can't she see he's after her money? He could do better than that. And so on. Or else what others see is a perfectly matched pair, a union made in heaven, and of course the couple has to live up to that, or else.

We project ourselves into their relationship, how we would feel if we were in their shoes.

Yes, I think so. That's a big subject, projection. It will come up a lot in this seminar—how we come to be attracted to someone, or maybe take an instant dislike, depending on what's being projected.

You see, Jung believed that everything about ourselves that we are not conscious of is projected onto someone else. This isn't an active process—we meet with projections, we don't make them. Just as we tend to assume that the world is as we see it, we naively suppose that other people are what we imagine them to be. "The mind in its natural state presupposes the existence of such projections," writes Jung. "It is the natural and given thing for unconscious contents to be projected."[5] So we see in others both our own worst features and our own undeveloped potential.

This isn't necessarily bad. If the projection is positive, it creates an agreeable bridge between people. It makes friendship possible and it's the meat and potatoes at social gatherings.

I think the best thing about projections is that we get to withdraw them! When we assume that some quality or characteristic is present in someone, and then through our experience of that person we discover they aren't really like that at all, we have a chance to become more conscious than we were. The little woman who won your heart

---

[5] "General Aspects of Dream Psychology," *The Structure and Dynamics of the Psyche,* CW 8, par. 507.

turns out to be a she-devil, the devoted breadwinner takes off with someone else. If we are at all reflective, we will question ourselves: What did I see in him? Why was I attracted to her in the first place? What blinded me to what that person was really like?

You can be deliberately fooled by another person, can't you? They can pretend to be what they aren't.

Sure, don't we all?! But who's responsible for what? There's always a hook, some trait or characteristic in me, part of my own make-up, that's also in the other person. I know a man who was bilked by a stockbroker, a real con man. My friend was stung for a few thousand dollars. Who do you blame? What led my friend to believe him in the first place? Many others didn't. One could say he projected his own "good neighbor." It was an expensive lesson.

Of course it works the other way round too—maybe we don't trust someone because we see the worst—our own shadow—where it isn't. Projection is like a two-way mirror, we see both the other person and a reflection of our own unacknowledged face. It's a misty mirror, it's not easy to tell who's who, and as a matter of fact Jung said there's no need to until or unless there's a disturbance in the relationship.

Can you project onto things?

Yes, that used to be called a fetish. I once had an analysand who had a thing about doorknobs. She was fascinated with them, they were numinous to her. She had a marvelous collection of doorknobs and she dreamt about them. She couldn't go into a house without touching every knob on every door in the place! Of course they had a symbolic meaning for her. It took her a long time to understand what that was, but it was there. Doorknobs had something to do with her! It was a revelation. I had a similar experience with elephants.[6]

There are group projections too. We can have certain ideas about a

---

[6] See *The Survival Papers: Anatomy of a Midlife Crisis* (Toronto: Inner City Books, 1988), pp. 66-67.

race or a nationality that are far from the truth for a particular person of that color or country. We regularly scapegoat others in all sorts of ways—tar them with our own feathers.[7] And dumb animals, well, we all know what our dog or cat is thinking . . .

What does it mean, to withdraw a projection?

You take back what's yours.

And how do you know what that is?

By introspection and differentiation. Differentiation means separating parts from a whole. When projections are in the air, we ourselves and the other person—or thing—are parts of a whole. That's the gestalt of the situation. When there's a positive projection onto another person, we feel like one—soul-mates, that kind of thing. Of course we aren't one, we're at least two and many more if you count all those other personalities in us, lurking in the background. We only realize that when our expectations are frustrated. Then we have to ask, "What did I expect? What does that say about *me?*"

Withdrawing projections can be painful and it doesn't happen overnight, but according to Jung it's fundamental to the process of becoming conscious.

Returning to the comment a few minutes ago, yes, projection is certainly a factor in our interest in the relationships of other people. You could call it projective identification. We identify with one or other of the pair, or maybe both, and respond to their situation as if we ourselves were in it. That's why we rejoice at weddings and take sides when our happily married friends split up.

Of course, the couple being projected upon is affected by all this. I think that's all part of the "pronounced influence" Jung refers to. The perceptions and opinions of those outside the relationship invariably have an effect on those who are in it. This can lead to a so-called persona marriage, a relationship based on putting up a good front. It's

---

[7] See Sylvia Brinton Perera, *The Scapegoat Complex: Toward a Mythology of Shadow and Guilt* (Toronto: Inner City Books, 1986).

not unusual for people to stay together just because they don't want to disappoint their friends and relatives, or because they're stuck in an image of themselves as the ideal couple.

You see already, in this first paragraph, there's enough material for a book!

So there are a lot of objective factors that result in friction between partners, but they're not what this essay is about. Jung deliberately chooses to disregard such things. Let us assume, or hope, he has bigger fish to fry. Here is what he says next:

> Whenever we speak of a "psychological relationship" we presuppose one that is *conscious,* for there is no such thing as a psychological relationship between two people who are in a state of unconsciousness. From the psychological point of view they would be wholly without relationship. (par. 325)

This is really a remarkable statement: *"There is no such thing as a psychological relationship between two people who are in a state of unconsciousness."* There are enormous implications in that, and analysts deal with them every day. Then Jung goes on:

> From any other point of view, the physiological for example, they could be regarded as related, but one could not call their relationship psychological.

What do you think Jung means by that, "physiological"? What would a physiological relationship look like?

I suppose something biological—good sex?

Well, that's one way to read it. Sexual compatibility can certainly be the cement of a good relationship, in the general sense of the word. And it's no secret that sexual frustration can lead to all kinds of acrimony and ill-considered behavior, from hurtful remarks to violence. People who feel good together in bed can experience an important connection and stay together a long time.

What about a celibate relationship, where the bond is spiritual?

Spiritual isn't biological, they're opposites.

I'd dispute that. Surely, when you look at the big picture, it's a continuum . . .

Of course, it's not unusual for people to have a spiritual connection because of their psychology. It happens every day. I'd be hard-pressed to say it was physiological, but even so, that wouldn't necessarily mean they had a psychological relationship.

Nor would good sex.

Yes, it's all up for grabs. Myself, I understand Jung to mean here that he's not concerned with the instinctual response of one person to another. You can include spiritual in that if you like, and celibacy too.[8] This essay is about what's behind all that. It's about relating *psychologically,* and for that to be possible, says Jung, the parties to the relationship have to be conscious.

Instinctual behavior is just that—innate, automatic. It has its own rhythm and there's nothing conscious about it. A man driven by his dick is unconscious. He comes and goes. Or maybe he stays. Who knows? Not the man himself because he's not in charge.

I wish my boyfriend could hear this.

We could say something similar about a woman longing for babies. She's driven by an instinctual urge, and so she's vulnerable to being impregnated by the first man to catch her fancy.

That was before birth control. Nowadays we can choose to become pregnant or not.

Yes, so I've heard. I grew up in the fifties, when you took your chances, but I don't think it's so much different today. How many unexpected—I won't say unwanted—pregnancies do you know of? A woman driven by her biological urge can only hope she makes a suitable choice, but as we all know, the choice is not necessarily ra-

---

[8] For a discussion of the psychology of celibate love, see John P. Dourley, *Love, Celibacy and the Inner Marriage* (Toronto: Inner City Books, 1987), pp. 25-43.

tional, which is to say conscious.

Did Jung have anything good to say about instinctual behavior?

Of course. He saw a real danger in getting out of touch with the instincts, becoming too "civilized." It's a fine line we're talking about. We are not only rational beings, we're also animals. Here's an interesting statement of Jung's:

> I believe that the spirit is a dangerous thing and I do not believe in its paramountcy. I believe only in the Word become flesh, in the spirit-filled body, where *yang* and *yin* are wedded into a living form.[9]

The instincts can lead people to connect, but what happens next? And why? These are the questions Jung is concerned with in this essay. In Jung's view, unexamined instinctual behavior is a hallmark of unconsciousness and a fundamental characteristic of the undeveloped mind. In a lecture at Harvard University in 1936, Jung says:

> An extreme state of unconsciousness is characterized by the predominance of compulsive instinctual processes, the result of which is either uncontrolled inhibition or a lack of inhibition throughout. . . . The unconscious is then found to be at a definitely animal level.[10]

And he contrasts this with what's involved in being conscious:

> A high degree of consciousness, on the other hand, is characterized by a heightened awareness, a preponderance of will, directed, rational behaviour, and an almost total absence of instinctual determinants.[11]

It's not unusual for Jung to take this position. One of his basic beliefs—maybe even his essential message—is that the purpose of human life is to become conscious. Part and parcel of this is achieving a balance between spirit and instinct. Go too far one way or the other and we get into trouble. Jung says it all in one sentence:

---

[9] "The Swiss Line in the European Spectrum," *Civilization in Transition,* CW 10, par. 917.

[10] "Psychological Factors in Human Behaviour," *The Structure and Dynamics of the Psyche,* CW 8, par. 249.

[11] Ibid.

Too much of the animal distorts the civilized man, too much civilization makes sick animals.[12]

On that note, let's take a break.

*

We were talking about consciousness, its importance to Jung and how being conscious differs from just living instinctually.

Some of you may be puzzled about what all this has to do with relationships, and I can only hope that will become clear as we go along. Right now we're looking at the foundation of the house of cards we all live in . . .

You see, the civilized man—and that's us, male or female—tends to live in his head. He prides himself on his rational approach to life, and rightly so. We are no longer apes. On the other hand, the more we lose touch with our other side, our instinctual base, the more likely it is that something will happen *in us* to bring about a better balance. This is the basis for Jung's idea of compensation within the psyche. One way or another, we'll be brought down to earth. It's just when we think we have everything under control that we are most apt to fall on our face. We get bigger than our boots when we don't reckon with the animal in us. In a so-called civilized person, the instincts are part of the shadow—we repress them, or hear their call and ignore it.

So an instinctual connection between people is no small thing. It's a strong message, one we should listen to. But let's not lose sight of what we gain by becoming conscious. This isn't just a theoretical issue, it has practical consequences. In a 1927 lecture Jung said:

> The reason why consciousness exists, and why there is an urge to widen and deepen it, is very simple: without consciousness things go less well.[13]

---

[12] "The Eros Theory," *Two Essays in Analytical Psychology*, CW 7, par. 32.

[13] "Analytical Psychology and 'Weltanschauung,' " *The Structure and Dynamics of the Psyche*, CW 8, par. 695.

Just ponder that—*"without consciousness things go less well"*—
and see where it takes you. Put it beside Jung's belief that the unexamined life is not worth living, and it seems to me you have in a nut-
shell Jung's motivation for all his work, not to mention a major reason for the current interest in it.

*Yes, but there are many schools of thought on what constitutes con-
sciousness.*

So there are. Here I can only tell you what Jung means by it, what he
has in mind when he talks about being conscious as opposed to being
"in a state of unconsciousness."

Jung defined consciousness as "the function or activity which
maintains the relation of psychic contents to the ego."[14] In that way
he distinguished it conceptually from the *psyche,* which is made up
of both consciousness and the unconscious. In Jung's model, the
ego isn't the same thing as consciousness, it's simply the central
complex of the conscious mind. Of course, in practice we can only
become aware of psychic contents by means of the ego—Jung says
that here in the next paragraph of the marriage essay: "So far as we
know, consciousness is always ego-consciousness." This means, in
effect, that the more we know about what's going on in our own
unconscious, the more conscious we are.

We live in a stream of events, something new happens to us every
day. Mostly, we're so caught up in routine that we don't even notice.
Consciousness is the result of reflecting on events instead of just reacting to them. Routine especially gets in the way of being conscious. We can sleepwalk through life as long as we stick to the tried
and true. Think about it. When were you last *surprised?*

I recently got a taste of what the unconscious can do to wake us
up. I'd agreed to give a Friday evening lecture and a Saturday seminar in Lafayette, Louisiana. I did this with some reluctance because I
don't like traveling, it interferes with my routine. Anyway, I booked
my flight three months in advance to get the cheapest fare, and I was

---

14 "Definitions," *Psychological Types,* CW 6, par. 700.

packed and ready to go two days before the flight. That too is routine for me. I pride myself on being attentive to details. I cross all the t's and dot all the i's.

It was an uneventful flight, and late Friday afternoon I stood outside the Lafayette airport waiting for my designated chauffeur. Nobody came and nobody came. After half an hour I began to notice all the passing cars had *Indiana* license plates . . .

Talk about your sinking heart!

How awful!

Didn't you check your ticket?

Of course, I don't take anything for granted! It said Lafayette, IN, but I thought that meant "in" as opposed to "out"—and I *was* going *in* to Lafayette . . .

I eventually got to Louisiana, about midnight. I went to bed feeling pretty low, but the next day I gave my talk and did the seminar and had a great time. It was really quite special. I'm still assimilating the meaning of that experience, but I like the perspective of the woman who was waiting to pick me up at the airport. This is from her letter to me after that weekend:

> Carson McCullers said, "Life is such a sudden place." I say this quite frequently and I think it even more. This is what I felt at the airport when you didn't show up. Even though I did use all of my October adrenalin, I had fun.
>
> You, it would seem, had the unique experience of knowing (even if just for one afternoon),
>
> where you were
> where you weren't, &
> where you were going to go.
>
> Now I ask you. And they say the unconscious doesn't have a sense of humor . . . [15]

I think that's as good an expression as any of what's involved in being conscious. My analyst once said something similar. "Think of

---

[15] Thanks to Sidney Creaghan of Acadiana Friends of Jung.

what you've been," he said, "what you are now, and then reflect on what you could be."

That's a tall order.

Yes, but even if you can manage that, it's only the start. Jung also believed that consciousness involves discriminating between opposites.[16] The basic opposites are ego-consciousness and the unconscious, so first of all you have to acknowledge that there *are* some things about yourself you're not aware of. And then you have to discriminate between a whole range of other opposites—like masculine and feminine, good and evil, and so on. Here, in this essay, Jung ties consciousness, and the possibility of relationship, to the capacity or ability to tell the difference between subject and object—oneself and somebody else:

> In order to be conscious of myself, I must be able to distinguish myself from others. Relationship can only take place where this distinction exists. (par. 326)

Elsewhere Jung describes two distinct ways in which consciousness arises.[17] One is during a moment of high emotional tension involving a situation in the outer world. Maybe we feel uneasy for no obvious reason, or strangely attracted to someone, and suddenly we see the meaning in what's going on. The other happens in a state of quiet contemplation, where ideas pass before the mind's eye like dream-images. Suddenly there's a flash of association between two apparently disconnected and widely separated ideas.

In each case it's the discharge of energy-tension that produces consciousness. These sudden realizations and flashes of insight are what we experience as revelations.

Where does consciousness come from?

---

[16] See, for instance, "Psychological Aspects of the Mother Archetype," *The Archetypes and the Collective Unconscious,* CW 9i, par. 178.

[17] "Analytical Psychology and Education," *The Development of Personality,* CW 17, par. 207.

In Jung's model of the psyche, consciousness is a kind of super-structure based on the unconscious and arising out of. Here's how he described it in a lecture in 1943:

> Consciousness does not create itself—it wells up from unknown depths. In childhood it awakens gradually, and all through life it wakes each morning out of the depths of sleep from an unconscious condition. It is like a child that is born daily out of the primordial womb of the unconscious. . . . It is not only influenced by the unconscious but continually emerges out of it in the form of numberless spontaneous ideas and sudden flashes of thought.[18]

In the marriage essay he uses a different metaphor:

> In the child, consciousness rises out of the depths of unconscious psychic life, at first like separate islands, which gradually unite to form a "continent," a continuous land-mass of consciousness. Progressive mental development means, in effect, extension of consciousness. (par. 326)

And then he restates his basic position: "With the rise of a continuous consciousness, and not before, psychological relationship becomes possible."

What do you think that means, "continuous consciousness"?

The difference between a child and an adult?

I think that's part of it. A child lives in a state of oneness with its mother, or the person who nowadays is called the primary caregiver. There's little separation between subject and object. As the growing child assimilates its experience, develops its own boundaries, its own sense of self separate from the outside world, so the ego comes into being. There's a recognizable sense of personal identity, an "I am." This goes on in fits and starts, until at some point you have this metaphorical land-mass, a continent of ego surrounded by the waters of the unconscious. Some of what was previously unconscious has become conscious.

---

[18] "The Psychology of Eastern Meditation," *Psychology and Religion,* CW 11, par. 935.

The first half of life generally involves this developmental process. If we get decent mirroring in the very early years, we stand a good chance of acquiring a healthy ego.[19] But as I pointed out a few minutes ago, having an ego is not the same thing as being conscious. There are lots of take-charge people with very strong egos—captains of industry, politicians and so on—who are still quite unconscious. I'd say this is the rule rather than the exception. You can be a leader, you can run things like a clock and know how to manage others. But if you don't have the time or interest to introspect, to question yourself, you can't claim to be conscious.

In fact, mature consciousness, according to Jung, is dependent on a working relationship between a strong but flexible ego and what he called the Self, the regulating center of the psyche. Of course for that to happen, the ego has to acknowledge that it isn't in charge. That cuts out the ego-maniacs! This isn't a natural process, it's a major shift in perspective, like the difference between thinking the earth is the center of the solar system and then finding out the sun is. It generally doesn't happen—if it ever does—until later in life. You get some experience under your belt and you look back and realize there was more going on than you knew. Something greater than you was pulling the strings. That's humbling and puts an end to inflation.

Is Self Jung's word for God?

Not exactly. It's the archetype of wholeness, a transpersonal power that transcends the ego. There's no essential difference between the Self as an experiential, psychological reality and the religious concept of a supreme being, but the traditional idea of God places him somewhere "out there." The Self is inside.

Becoming conscious, then, is a continuous process, *by* the ego, of assimilating what was previously unknown *to* the ego. It involves a progressive waking up to why we do what we do. And a major step

---

[19] See Nathan Schwartz-Salant, *Narcissism and Character Transformation: The Psychology of Narcissistic Character Disorders* (Toronto: Inner City Books, 1982), pp. 45ff.

is to become aware of the many ways we're influenced by unconscious aspects of ourselves.

Now, who among us would admit to being unconscious?!

I suppose we all are, to some extent.

Yes, I think we can't escape it. Being conscious is not a question of
IQ. It has very little to do with how smart we are, or the accumula-
tion of knowledge—how much we know. It's a completely subjective phenomenon. It depends on how much we know about *ourselves*. Although, as Jung points out here, no one is ever totally unconscious, on the other hand we are only ever *relatively* conscious—
compared to what we were before.

Jung compared the unconscious to an ocean, because both are vast
and inexhaustible. Freud saw the unconscious, or subconscious, as
little more than a garbage can of fantasies and emotions that were active when we were children and then were repressed or forgotten. To
this day, classical psychoanalysis is based on that premise. Jung
bought all that for a while. He was an early champion of Freud's
theories and for a few years they were close friends.[20] But in the end
he couldn't swallow the dogma, it just didn't accord with his own
experience.

Jung came to believe that in fact the unconscious also includes
contents we never knew were there. Things about ourselves, in our
personal unconscious, and then at a deeper level—what Jung called
the collective unconscious—all the varied experiences of the human
race, the stuff of myths and religion and fairy tales. Under the right
circumstances, any of this can become conscious.

In his essay "On the Nature of the Psyche," Jung says,

> The unconscious is not simply the unknown, it is rather the *un-
> known psychic.*[21]

---

20 See *Freud and Psychoanalysis,* CW 4, and *The Freud/Jung Letters: The
Correspondence between Sigmund Freud and C.G. Jung* (Bollingen Series
XCIV), trans. Ralph Manheim and R.F.C. Hull, ed. William McGuire (Princeton: Princeton University Press, 1974).
21 *The Structure and Dynamics of the Psyche,* CW 8, par. 382.

The "unknown psychic" is Jung's catch-all for everything in the psyche—consciousness and the unconscious, the two together—that isn't currently related to, or known by, the ego. Jung goes on to give a partial list of unconscious contents as follows:

> Everything of which I know, but of which I am not at the moment thinking; everything of which I was once conscious but have now forgotten; everything perceived by my senses, but not noted by my conscious mind; everything which, involuntarily and without paying attention to it, I feel, think, remember, want, and do; all the future things that are taking shape in me and will sometime come to consciousness: all this is the content of the unconscious.[22]

That doesn't leave much out!

Yes, no wonder something new is always coming up! And that's why we'll always be more or less unconscious. The way I see it, we're all prisoners of our own psychology, but if we work on ourselves enough and get lucky, we might make day parole . . .

We seem to have got off the topic, or else I'm in the wrong place. My wife is interested in another man and my kids are out half the night. I just don't know what to do . . . I was hoping I'd get some answers here.

I'm sorry, there are no quick fixes. You can't understand what's going on between you and your wife, or why your kids would rather be somewhere else, until you know what's happening in you. What they're up to may have nothing to do with you—or everything! There's no way to know until you yourself are more conscious. When you have yourself in hand, when you know where you stand and why, then you'll know what to do. That may take some personal therapy.

We're bound to talk theory here, and you have to decide if and how it applies to you. This isn't the proper forum for specific personal problems. We came together to discuss what's generally in-

---

[22] Ibid.

volved in the psychology of relationships. Well, we're circumambulating the subject. That gives us lots of leeway.

Circum . . . ?

Walking around it.

We have *strayed from Jung's essay.*

Yes, but that's the way it goes when you talk about psychological issues. You start off with X and in two minutes you're deep in Y, and then Z comes up! It's like that in analysis too. A man comes in preoccupied with a problem at work. That's all he has in mind, it's the only thing he wants to talk about. He plops himself down and before you know it he's in tears about something that happened in Grade Two! And it turns out to be right on the point of what's happening at work! And he ends up talking about his mother! You can't compartmentalize the psyche, it confounds us every time.

Now, after noting that the ability to distinguish oneself from others is the essential precondition of consciousness, Jung ends paragraph 326 with this observation:

> Although the distinction may be made in a general way, normally it is incomplete, because large areas of psychic life still remain unconscious. As no distinction can be made with regard to unconscious contents, on this terrain no relationship can be established; here there still reigns the original unconscious condition of the ego's primitive identity with others, in other words a complete absence of relationship.

Do you see what he's saying? To the extent that we're still unconscious of ourselves, so we are limited in our ability to relate psychologically to another person.

Let me put it another way: whatever aspects of ourselves we're not conscious of, we're apt to see in someone else. The question is, are we then relating to that person at all, or to an unconscious side of ourselves? If we don't see the reality of the other person, we're trapped in a narcissistic bubble.

What is meant by primitive identity?

Jung used the term primitive to refer to the original, undifferentiated human psyche—a state of oneness with the surroundings. It's virtually the same thing as calling something archaic, which means primal or original. And the term identity, psychologically, means an unconscious conformity between subject and object.

Jung borrowed an expression from anthropology to describe all this—*participation mystique.*[23] It's the basis for projection and identification—not knowing where the subject—that's me—ends, and the object—someone else—begins. Here is Jung:

> Identity is responsible for the naïve assumption that the psychology of one man is like that of another, that the same motives occur everywhere, that what is agreeable to me must obviously be pleasurable for others, that what I find immoral must also be immoral for them, and so on. It is also responsible for the almost universal desire to correct in others what most needs correcting in oneself.[24]

Of course we all fall into this from time to time. We can't help it because we're never as conscious or civilized as we think we are. There are always aspects of ourselves that are outside our ken. As Jung says in the next paragraph of the marriage essay,

> We constantly overestimate the existing content of consciousness, and it is a great and surprising discovery when we find that what we had supposed to be the final peak is nothing but the first step in a very long climb. (par. 327)

If we're always more or less unconscious, it's hard to see how a psychological relationship is possible at all . . .

Yes, it does seem problematic. I should say that according to Jung's essay the chances get worse before they get better!

So far we've learned that consciousness is the basic requirement for a psychological relationship. As a matter of fact, Jung went a lot

---

[23] "Definitions," *Psychological Types,* CW 6, par. 741.
[24] Ibid., par. 742.

further than that. He believed that individual consciousness was necessary in order for God himself to become conscious . . . He writes about this in *Answer to Job,* which some people think is his most important work.[25]

We've run out of time, so I'll have to leave that for you to explore yourselves.

---

[25] "Answer to Job," *Psychology and Religion,* CW 11. See also Edward F. Edinger, *The Creation of Consciousness: Jung's Myth for Modern Man* (Toronto: Inner City Books, 1984), chapter 4, "The Transformation of God," and Edinger, *Transformation of the God-Image: An Elucidation of Jung's* Answer to Job (Toronto: Inner City Books, 1992).

Seminar Two

Before we start, are there any questions about last week's material?

Is there such a thing as a relationship not influenced by projection?

In Jung's terms, by definition, no. Since we can only ever be relatively conscious, there's always something about ourselves that we're liable to project. So, for instance, we fall in love yet again, and yet again we're disappointed. It wasn't *quite* what we wanted, or not what we were looking for at all. You don't have to know anything about psychology to know when a relationship just doesn't work. But why doesn't it? How did you get yourself into it in the first place? And what do you do now? That's psychology.

Jung says that whatever we're unconscious of in ourselves, we will meet in the outside world, as fate. There's always a reason for what happens to us. Of course we may not know it at the time! How could we? Only by living it out, accepting what comes and then reflecting on it, can we find the meaning of our life.

No perfect relationships?

It depends on what you mean by perfect. Some men have a fantasy of a so-called omni-available woman.[26] She's adoring, understanding and always ready to make love. She's attentive to his every mood. She wants only him, his every word is gospel and she never rejects him. He could cry on her shoulder one minute and screw her brains out the next.

Mother and lover all rolled up into one.

Yes, would that make for a perfect relationship? I imagine women have their own idea of an omni-available man.

---

[26] See Warren Steinberg, *Circle of Care: Clinical Issues in Jungian Therapy* (Toronto: Inner City Books, 1990), p. 99.

He'd always be there and he'd love to cook and cuddle and do the laundry!

He'd know when I wasn't in the mood.

He'd give me space.

There you are. And would that be perfect, or simply convenient? Jung often said perfection is reserved for the gods. The rest of us have to muddle along as best we can. Gods know everything. We humans are limited by what we don't know about ourselves.

Mind you, between what's desirable and what's unattainable, we may chance upon what is workable. Do you remember that Rolling Stones song, "You Can't Always Get What You Want"? There's a line there, something like, "but if you try, somehow, you just might get what you need . . ." A perfectly workable relationship—I mean one that's harmonious and relatively conflict-free—is possible, given partners that don't expect perfection . . .

Of course, to be satisfied with anything less than perfection already presumes a degree of psychological maturity, which is essentially what's involved in Jung's fundamental statement: "There is no such thing as a psychological relationship between two people who are in a state of unconsciousness."

If we got everything we wanted from a relationship we wouldn't need to know anything about psychology.

Or be conscious, either! Now, let's look at paragraph 327:

> The young person of marriageable age does, of course, possess an ego-consciousness (girls more than men, as a rule), but, since he has only recently emerged from the mists of original unconsciousness [that's the "primitive identity" we talked about last time], he is certain to have wide areas which still lie in the shadow and which preclude to that extent the formation of psychological relationship. This means, in practice, that the young man (or woman) can have only an incomplete understanding of himself and others, and is therefore imperfectly informed as to his, and their, motives. As a rule the motives he acts from are largely unconscious. Subjectively, of course,

he thinks himself very conscious and knowing, for we constantly overestimate the existing content of consciousness, and it is a great and surprising discovery when we find that what we had supposed to be the final peak is nothing but the first step in a very long climb. The greater the area of unconsciousness, the less is marriage a matter of free choice, as is shown subjectively in the fatal compulsion one feels so acutely when one is in love. The compulsion can exist even when one is not in love, though in less agreeable form.

To my mind, the important points here are Jung's reference to the shadow and the idea of free choice as opposed to compulsion. In the next paragraph he expands on what he means by unconscious motives, so I'd like to focus first on what is involved in Jung's notion of the shadow, and then on what lies behind what he refers to as a fatal compulsion.

Now, what do you know about the shadow?

It's our dark side.

The things about ourselves we don't like.

The evil that men do . . . And women too, of course.

Yes, all that, and much, much more. Remember what I said last time about the unconscious not being just a garbage can? Jung describes the shadow as all those hidden or unconscious aspects of oneself, both good and bad, that the ego has either repressed or never been aware of at all. Everything about yourself that you aren't conscious of is shadow, which means that before unconscious contents have been differentiated, separated out, the shadow is in effect the whole of the unconscious. The less you know about yourself, the more unconscious you are, and therefore the more of you is shadow.

On the negative side, the shadow is made up of repressed desires and uncivilized impulses, morally inferior motives, childish fantasies, resentments and so on—all those things about ourselves we're not proud of.

We've talked about how our own inclinations, when we're not aware of them, can be experienced in other people. What we don't know about ourselves, we meet in others. That's the natural process of projection. Think of someone you don't like, and ask yourself what it is about that person you can't stand—someone you've caught in a lie, say, or a man who's cheated on his wife, a friend who's a two-faced gossip, whatever.

Think about it. Reflect on yourself with a critical eye and see if you can recognize something of what they are, what they've done, in yourself. Are you always truthful, completely honest? Did you ever crib somebody's notes for an essay, fudge an expense account, not declare some income on your tax return? Did you ever bad-mouth a friend behind their back? No? Wouldn't you *like* to?

Not acknowledging your shadow makes you prudish and self-righteous. You're above it all, godlike. Your motives are pure, your conscience is perfectly clear. It's everybody else who's at fault.

There's no mote in my *eye . . .*

Yes, go far enough with that and you're deep in paranoia, everybody's out to get you. This isn't a good basis for *any* relationship, let alone one based on consciousness. Here's how Jung puts it:

> The shadow is a moral problem that challenges the whole ego-personality, for no one can become conscious of the shadow without considerable moral effort. To become conscious of it involves recognizing the dark aspects of the personality as present and real.[27]

And he goes on:

> Although, with insight and good will, the shadow can to some extent be assimilated into the conscious personality, experience shows that there are certain features which offer the most obstinate resistance to moral control and prove almost impossible to influence. These resistances are usually bound up with *projections*, which are not recognized as such, and their recognition is a moral achievement beyond the ordinary. While some traits peculiar to the shadow can be recognized without too much difficulty as one's own personal qualities, in this case both insight and good will are unavailing because

---

[27] "The Shadow," *Aion,* CW 9ii, par. 14.

the cause of the emotion appears to lie, beyond all possibility of doubt, in the *other person.*[28]

You said there was some good in the shadow?

Yes, it also consists of abilities and moral qualities that we haven't realized in ourselves. Here's Jung:

> The shadow is merely somewhat inferior, primitive, unadapted, and awkward; not wholly bad. It even contains childish or primitive qualities which would in a way vitalize and embellish human existence, but—convention forbids![29]

And again:

> If it has been believed hitherto that the human shadow was the source of all evil, it can now be ascertained on closer investigation that the unconscious man, that is, his shadow, does not consist only of morally reprehensible tendencies, but also displays a number of good qualities, such as normal instincts, appropriate reactions, realistic insights, creative impulses, etc.[30]

How do you assimilate the shadow?

By becoming more conscious of who you are, what you're capable of. Think of the worst thing you've ever done. Don't worry, you don't have to tell us! And then think of what you'd really like to do, what you've never dared, say, because of what people might think. Those are the two sides of the shadow.

There's no formal technique for assimilating the shadow. Jung says it's more like diplomacy or statesmanship, and it's always an individual matter. First you have to accept its existence. There's a side of you that's not like you at all, at least not the "you" you'd like to think of yourself as, not the "you" you want others to see. Personify it, give it a name—Norman, Nancy, whatever. Second, you have to get to know the qualities and intentions of your shadow,

---

[28] Ibid., par. 16.
[29] "Psychology and Religion," *Psychology and Religion,* CW 11, par. 134.
[30] "Conclusion," *Aion,* CW 9ii, par. 423.

what it looks like and what it wants. You do this by paying attention to your moods and fantasies. You talk to your Norman or Nancy to find out where their energy wants to go. That's what Jung called active imagination. Listen to what he says:

> This process of coming to terms with the Other in us is well worth while, because in this way we get to know aspects of our nature which we would not allow anybody else to show us and which we ourselves would never have admitted.[31]

Do you see? Nobody is One. We can't ignore our other side.

I'm sorry, I don't know what you mean.

I'm afraid you lost me too.

Sorry? Afraid? My goodness! You're paying for this . . .

I'll give you a personal example. When my niece got married a few years ago I was asked to toast the bride. I liked the guy she was marrying, but I couldn't see why she did. She was pretty conventional and he was anything but. He never had a steady job, he spent his time with drinking buddies and planning his next big score. He was a tear-ass and a con-man, is what he was, he lived on the edge. I knew all that, but what can you do, he was her choice.

The wedding was a posh affair at a local golf club. I got all dressed up and had my little speech ready. When it came my turn, I said the usual things about what she was like when she was little and oh my, wasn't she something now! And then, right out of the blue, I found myself saying not nice things about her new husband. That he was an ill-disguised thug, a king-pin in the local drug trade, that his fondest wish was to have a wife with a regular salary, how he'd never amount to anything, and on and on.

I made a joke of all this, but it didn't go over very well. His parents were completely spooked. My niece let it pass and her new husband laughed it off, but I couldn't sleep that night.

How could I, a perfect gentleman, always polite and concerned to

---

[31] "The Conjunction," *Mysterium Coniunctionis,* CW 14, par. 706.

do the right thing, do just the opposite? The answer lies in my shadow. Where I'm concerned to put on a good front, as most of us are, he doesn't give a shit.

It wasn't the first time my shadow had spoken his mind. In one of my books I tell about how he dumped a bowl of salad on a lady's head.[32] And once he threw up when I was being interviewed for a job! In some ways he's also more truthful than me. Two years after that wedding, my niece's husband took off, leaving her with a child and a pile of bills. And he owed me a thousand dollars!

You see, when you get too high and mighty, full of "the right stuff," the shadow brings you down to earth—cuts you off at the knees. The more we pride ourselves on being civilized—polite and rational—the more there builds up an explosive drive to say or do something that reflects how you really feel. That's shadow. Until we know about it, of course. When we know about it, when we consciously acknowledge it's there, it becomes an aspect of our personality. That's assimilation—the integration of unconscious contents into consciousness.

I remember the film Network, *with Faye Dunaway and Peter Finch. He's an executive with a big television network and he gradually sees the hypocrisy of it all. It's a terrific film. The climax is where he shouts out the window: "I'm fed up and I'm not going to take it anymore!"*

Yes, that's a revolt of the shadow. And if *you* go on saying "I'm sorry . . ." or "I'm afraid . . . ," when you're really feeling pissed off that what I say doesn't make sense, why this room will become a powder keg!

Is the shadow always the very opposite of the ego and how we consciously see ourselves?

Not necessarily. More often it compensates—a little bit here, a little

---

[32] *The Survival Papers: Anatomy of a Midlife Crisis* (Toronto: Inner City Books, 1988), p. 81.

bit there. We're seldom so one-sided, so blinkered, that we don't know anything at all about our shadow.

But you see, most of us have developed a persona to deal with the world. We have a conventional mask. It helps us get along with other people. There's nothing wrong with that, it's a convenient social fiction. For instance, I know your occupations, but what *else* are you? What's your motivation for being here? I imagine that's more important than your social position.

The persona protects our privacy and most people aren't interested in who we really are anyway. There's only a problem when we *identify* with the persona—when we come to believe that's all we are. Then the shadow steps in. "No," says the shadow, "I'm here too, you are also *this.*" Then we get clobbered by the opposite.

What's the difference between the ego and the persona?

Well, sometimes nothing at all! At least not when you identify with your social role, your public face, like being a teacher or a wife or a priest. But who's behind that? Who are you without your mask?

In Jung's model of the psyche, the ego and the persona are both functional complexes. The ego, you may remember, is the central complex of consciousness.[33] The persona is simply what we show to the outside world, usually ideal aspects of ourselves. It's a complex that comes into being as a way of adapting to our surroundings. That's why it's called functional, it facilitates how we function . . .

Is it who I am, my personality?

No, your personality, the real you, is generally obscured by the persona . . . well, more or less.

And the ego's the real you.

No, the ego is just those aspects of yourself you're aware of. Don't forget the shadow. And there's the anima and animus, of course, we haven't talked about them yet. They can turn you upside down! Not

---

[33] See above, p. 18.

to mention all the other complexes . . .

It's enough to make you scream!

Where does individuality come in?

What does all this have to do with relationship? . . .

I think it's important to deal with what comes up here. We can always come back to the essay . . .

Please. Let's just slow down and see if we can sort this sort. I don't think we're off the track at all. Everything we've been talking about is involved in being conscious, and consciousness, in Jung's terms, is the *sine qua non* of a psychological relationship.

What's sinnykwanon?

It's Latin for without which not.

Not which what?

It means you can't have one without the other.

Okay. So we all have a social identity, that's what we call a persona. Jung described the persona as an aspect of the collective psyche. That means there's nothing individual about it. It can *feel* individual—don't we all feel unique and special?—but the descriptions of us from the outside, "mother," "teacher," "doctor" and so on, don't describe a particular person. They don't distinguish one doctor or mother or teacher from any other.

What do you think does?

My attitude, the way I feel?

Our personal experience?

Yes, all that. The persona is a surface thing. As I said, it's useful and it's a way to keep our distance, but we all know there's more to us than other people see.

And how does the persona affect a relationship?

Well, there's the kind of marriage I mentioned last time, where the partners are attached to an image of themselves as the perfect couple, or they put on a good front for their friends. They'll even pretend to their spouse, anything not to spoil the illusion.

I had an analysand who saw himself as a dedicated family man. That was his persona. He was desperately unhappy, but he wouldn't dare tell his wife. He knew she was having an affair and he felt awful, but he put up with it because he was civilized and rational. That too was persona. He finally left the marriage, but it took years, and before he could make a move he had to get to know his shadow.

You see, we have to be able to drop our persona in situations where it isn't appropriate. In intimate relationships it just gets in the way. I'm an analyst and I publish books, but that's not who I am when I'm playing poker with my daughter or snooker with my son. The doctor who identifies with his function as a healer is just a pain in the butt to his neglected mate. The wise preacher leaves his collar and his rhetoric in the vestry when he goes out courting.

In matters of the heart, it's quite common to be attracted to what we see on the surface. But getting hooked up with someone because of that, their persona, is like buying a pig in a poke. We're definitely in for some surprises! You can fall in love with a persona, but it's just a shell, so of course you can't relate to it . . .

There was a question about individuality. Jung says that until the persona has been differentiated from the ego—before you know the difference between the way other people see you and how you really feel yourself to be—the persona *is* experienced as individuality. In fact, as a social identity on the one hand and an ideal image on the other, there's almost nothing that's individual about it. The persona is a mask that *feigns* individuality, it makes us believe we're individual when we're really only acting a role. Here's what Jung writes:

> When we analyse the persona we strip off the mask, and discover that what seemed to be individual is at bottom collective. . . . Fundamentally the persona is nothing real: it is a compromise between individual and society as to what a man should appear to be. He takes a name, earns a title, exercises a function, he is this or that.

> In a certain sense all this is real, yet in relation to the essential indi-
> viduality of the person concerned it is only a secondary reality, a
> compromise formation, in making which others often have a greater
> share than he.[34]

Do you understand that?

He, he . . . it's always he *with Jung. Why not* she? *What about me,*
women?

In this context, "he" is a genderless pronoun, it's generic for any
person, man or woman.

Generic refers to a class or group with things in common. Men and
women aren't generic.

Yes, there's certainly a profound difference between the sexes. Jung
wouldn't argue with that. But his language, the way he expressed
himself, was tied to the old school.

That's patriarchal!

So we say today.

I would have thought Jung was more conscious.

Well . . . using "he" like this is linguistically traditional . . .

That's no excuse.

I meant it as an explanation.

*Man*kind, hu*manity,* chair*man, it really makes me sick . . .*

Look, this language thing comes up all the time. We're a lot more
sensitive to these things than people were fifty years ago, even
twenty. And if you get testy about it, well, I'll tell you, you'd better
stay away from just about everything ever written that got us to
where we are—mythology, poetry, the Bible, you name it. What we

---

34 "The Persona as a Segment of the Collective Psyche," *Two Essays in*
Analytical Psychology, CW 7, par. 246.

have, the way we live—virtually everything we know as civilization—is built on a patriarchal foundation.

Socrates was a sexist pig. Copernicus too.

The past is done. If we trash it, if we disown the great thinkers of the
past because they didn't have our mind-set, why, we'd have to start
all over from scratch!

Not a bad idea.

*I don't think we can dismiss Jung's ideas just because he's sexist.
That would be* ad hominem.

Ad . . . ?

Let's hear him out.

I agree.

Me too.

I think it's time for a break.

*

Let's look at the overall picture. Ego, persona, shadow. In Jung's
model of the psyche, these are three major complexes among a whole
lot of others. Each has a say in what we are, the way we function,
the way we move through the world. The big question is, what do
they have to do with a psychological relationship?

You'll recall, at the end of paragraph 327, Jung refers to the fatal
compulsion that takes over when we fall in love. And of course we
can also fall into hate. In the background, pulling the strings, are
complexes. When our compulsive feelings are directed toward a person of the opposite sex, the particular complexes operating are generally what Jung called the anima, a man's internal image of woman,
or the animus, a woman's inner image of man. If our feelings are
tied up in a person of the same sex, more likely we're projecting
some aspect of our own shadow.

I think the most important thing to understand about complexes is that they determine how we feel and what we do—they deny us freedom of choice. We're not the master, or mistress, in our own house. Listen to Jung:

> Complexes interfere with the intentions of the will and disturb the conscious performance; they produce disturbances of memory and blockages in the flow of associations; they appear and disappear according to their own laws; they can temporarily obsess consciousness, or influence speech and action in an unconscious way. In a word, complexes behave like independent beings.[35]

Excuse me, what exactly is a complex?

Jung describes a complex as a bundle of energy associated with an idea, a mental image. Behind an affect, and that means any emotional reaction, you can be sure there's a complex.

That's going pretty far. Joy? Anger? Grief?

Everything. What makes you sad, what makes you glad. Why are some people happy about some things and others aren't? Why do you blow up at a remark that doesn't bother somebody else? Would you grieve for something or someone that meant nothing to you? It all comes down to your personal psychology, and that's where complexes come in.

Jung said that complexes are like islands in the psyche, split off from the ego-mainland. When you're emotional, caught up in a complex, you're on an island, so to speak, cut off from rational ego resources. The complex is in charge of what you say and do. When the storm dies down you swim ashore and lick your wounds, wondering what came over you. And sometimes you can't even remember what happened! It's like you had another personality that suddenly came alive. That's called dissociation, and when it's extreme—when the ego's too weak to hold things together—it's schizophrenia.

---

[35] "Psychological Factors in Human Behaviour," *The Structure and Dynamics of the Psyche,* CW 8, par. 253.

Of course, we generally don't look for a complex behind a good mood. Say you get some exciting news and jump for joy. Strictly speaking, you're complexed, but so what? There's no motivation to analyze it. On the other hand, if you fall in love and after a few days in seventh heaven it all goes sour, or maybe your boss gets on your nerves and you blow up and lose your job, well, you'd be wise to get to know what complex was behind it.

Are we born with complexes?

No, they develop after birth, according to our particular experience in the world. Mind you, there are templates, what Jung called the archetypes, patterns of behavior known and experienced by humans since the beginning of time. The psyche of the new-born child is not empty, it's not a *tabula rasa*.

Tabula . . . ?

A blank slate.

The archetypes are there when we're born, and so are the instincts, they're all part of our genetic make-up. The complexes, reflecting our own personal experience, build up around the archetypes.

Picture a ball. Complexes are on the surface and inside, at the core, are the archetypes. The templates, these archetypes, are there right from the start. You can't see them, but their effects turn up in the images and motifs that are the subject matter of religions, mythology, fairy tales and so on.

Popular songs too, and novels and art . . .

Yes. In our personal lives, they manifest as complexes that dictate certain patterns of behavior. We're all human, we have certain things in common. Some of that is instinctual, some archetypal. What's individual about us, truly our own, are our complexes.

Take the mother complex. It's determined mostly by your experience of your own mother, what that felt like.

I loved my mother, we were always very close.

Mine beat me black and blue. I hate her.

We've all had our own experience of mother. Maybe it was good, maybe not. Good or bad, it's part of what we are, that's our mother complex. But behind that—at the core of the complex—is the mother archetype, an inherited sense of all the possible experiences of "mother." The same is true of a father complex or any other. Archetypes include the opposites—mothers can be nurturing *or* angry, receptive *or* rejecting, and so on, and sometimes, in our personal lives, we get very mixed messages. The archetypes are just outlines of what's possible. Complexes are the coloring in.

Myths and fairy tales are full of archetypal patterns—they reflect the experience of the human race. That's why they're so helpful in figuring out the meaning of images, in a dream, say, or one that just pops into your head. The personal meaning of a particular image can be worked on either way. You can start with the archetype, the big picture, and see how it applies to you. Or work back, from the immediate emotional experience of the complex—a dream image or your reaction to something that happened—and see how it's related to an archetypal pattern.

Is a negative complex worse than a positive complex?

Worse? Not necessarily. Good, bad, worse, better—these are value judgments. A complex in itself is neutral. It's the *consequences* that can be called good or bad. A complex is just something that's constellated in certain situations.

Constellated?

That's when the complex becomes active. Think of a complex as an image or idea associated with certain feelings. When it's constellated, you're bound to react in a certain way. You literally have no choice. It's generally quite predictable. And if *we* don't know it, our friends sure do! "Don't mention his sister, she drives him up the wall." "Stay away from such-and-such, she just gets upset." "He can't think straight when you mention his father." We all have our own hot buttons. You can't have a rational conversation with someone caught in a complex. The best you can do is back off!

Of course complexes aren't always destructive, sometimes they're just boring. Did you ever find yourself at a party talking to a stamp collector or an avid bird-watcher? You could be stuck there all night! If you don't share their enthusiasm—I mean, if you don't have a similar complex—you just feel talked at.

Here's what Jung says about constellate:

> This term simply expresses the fact that the outward situation releases a psychic process in which certain contents gather together and prepare for action. When we say that a person is "constellated" we mean that he has taken up a position from which he can be expected to react in a quite definite way. . . . The constellated contents are definite complexes possessing their own specific energy.[36]

You see, ideas and images are like pinpoints of light in the psyche—similar to constellations of stars in the sky. That's where the term comes from.

What does it mean that complexes have their own specific energy?

It's just a way of saying that the energy bound up with the complex knows where it wants to go.

Coming back to the effect of a complex, negative or positive, good or bad. If, say, a man's experience of his personal mother was good—if she was receptive and attentive to his needs—we could say he has a positive mother complex. But maybe the consequences wouldn't be so good. He might go through life expecting just *that* kind of love, and always be frustrated. Whenever he met a woman who didn't live up to his early experience, he'd feel uncomfortable. If he didn't get from her what he wanted—as he did from his mother—he'd react to her as if she were a "bad" mother. You can imagine the effect on a relationship, which of course is further complicated because the woman he's involved with has her own experience, her own complexes . . .

---

[36] "A Review of the Complex Theory," ibid., par. 198.

A positive mother complex can sap a man's energy. Others don't generally accept him as readily or so unconditionally as his mother did. The world at large, where people are judged by what they do, is not positive mother. That can be quite a shock to a man who grew up being accepted at face value. On the other hand, he might excel in an institutional setting, the church, say, or a large corporation or maybe the civil service—jobs that simulate positive mother, with generous benefits and pension plans and long-term security. Would that be good or bad?

And what of the rejecting, bitchy woman who has no time for her kids? That image, of the negative mother, is there too, it's lying in wait even if you never knew it personally because it's part of the archetype, humanity's experience of "mother."

The other side of this coin is the man with a so-called negative mother complex. He might be forever suspicious of women, and especially those who wanted to take care of him—"good" mothers—but on the other hand he might respond very well to a woman who'd give him what he never had. Is that good or bad? And when you get right down to it, who's to say?

I suppose the man himself.

Yes, I think so. Sure, his friends would probably have an opinion! But since the effect of a complex is subjective, it can only really be judged from the inside.

You don't go looking to fix what feels good.

Exactly. So you see, the kind of complex you start off with, positive or negative, isn't the end of the story. The effects of complexes are a mixed bag. It's how you live them out that counts—what you make of what you got, added to what you picked up along the way. Of course, consciousness plays a part. That's what analysis is all about. Your reactions can be curbed if you're aware of your complexes. Get to know your complexes, areas where you're defensive or overly sensitive, and it's a whole new ball game.

Does analysis get rid of complexes?

No, by definition that's not possible. Complexes are the building blocks of the psychc, just like atoms and molecules make up tables and chairs. Without complexes, you don't exist. The question is whether they're active or not—how and when they get constellated—and how they affect your life. Those are the bread and butter issues in analysis.

But you don't try to get rid of them?

Can a leopard lose its spots? Without your complexes, you wouldn't be you. Your personality is the result of your complexes. You don't choose them and you can't get rid of them. The most you can do is understand their effects and work at depotentiating the ones that give you trouble.

Depotentiate?

Depotentiating a complex means taking away its power, loosening its influence. When you get to know your complexes, you have a better understanding of who you are and more control over how that's expressed—what you say and do, and so on. For instance, you have an emotional reaction but you don't have to blurt it out. You can hold back and reflect on it. Now just where did *that* come from? What came over me?

Depotentiating complexes is the result of becoming conscious of them. It doesn't happen overnight, it evolves over a period of time by asking yourself, time and time again—after, say, a heated exchange, an argument, that kind of thing—What got into me? Who was speaking? What got my goat?

The meat of a goat, incidentally, was the original sacrifice to the gods, in hopes of averting catastrophe. Later it was people who were sacrificed, "scapegoats"—they bore the brunt for the emotions people couldn't cope with—guilt, shame and so on.[37]

---

[37] See above, note 7.

My cousin keeps goats, he says they're cleaner than pigs . . .

What happens if you do nothing about your complexes, I mean if you don't know about them?

What doesn't? Wife beating, child abuse, relationship problems of every kind. That's just the tip of the iceberg. You can read about it every day, in every newspaper, in every country. Rape, murder, suicide, war. You could say that news is what happens when someone is complexed. Well, it's not news to me. Complexes aren't always troublesome, but some are bombs waiting to go off.

Everyone knows nowadays that people have complexes. What isn't so well known is that *complexes can have us.* But that's normal, and Jung says as much:

> To have complexes does not necessarily indicate inferiority. It only means that something discordant, unassimilated, and antagonistic exists, perhaps as an obstacle, but also as an incentive to greater effort, and so, perhaps, to new possibilities of achievement.[38]

Complexes work both ways, you see. They can stimulate us to greater consciousness and the better use of our abilities, or they can tie us up in knots. As long as we don't know about them, we're at their mercy.

Then we're neurotic.

Possibly, but not necessarily. Here . . . Jung says:

> The possession of complexes does not in itself signify neurosis . . . and the fact that they are painful is no proof of pathological disturbance. Suffering is not an illness; it is the normal counterpole to happiness. A complex becomes pathological only when we think we have not got it.[39]

The old adage, Know Thyself . . .

---

[38] "A Psychological Theory of Types," *Psychological Types,* CW 6, par. 925.
[39] "Psychotherapy and a Philosophy of Life," *The Practice of Psychotherapy,* CW 16, par. 179.

Yes, but the Greeks didn't know the half of it. They knew only of the conscious mind. The vast area of psychic activity we now call the unconscious was not even conceived of in those days. Complexes are by definition more or less unconscious, so they're always liable to boil up. Analysis can take the steam out of them to some extent, but some complexes you just learn to live with. It's like they're little devils hiding in the woodwork. One way or another, no matter how conscious you think you are, they always get you.

You can work on your feelings about a former lover for years, but still, whenever you run into her, or him, you're on edge, you're not yourself. You can analyze every detail of a miserable childhood and still get the jitters when you see your parents. That's the reality of the psyche. Getting to know your complexes doesn't make you invulnerable, but at least it prepares you for what to expect.

Next week we'll take a closer look at how our parental complexes affect a psychological relationship.

Interlude

"Moving right along," mused Rachel.

I bowed. "Thanks to you."

Rachel bit into a piece of cinnamon toast and licked her fingers. "You who? I'm you, that's who. It was your idea."

She picked up her book, a recent biography of Shen Li, an ancient Chinese sage.

I hung around.

Rachel looked up. "Yes?"

"Sometimes it's frustrating . . . To understand X you have to know Y. That leads to Z, which involves P. That takes you to E and M. Before you know it you're caught up in J . . . Help!"

Rachel touched my arm. "It's okay," she said, "I'm here."

I paced the room, silent.

"There's something else?" said Rachel, fingering Shen Li.

"Well . . . why does it take so long for me to write a book?"

Rachel shrugged.

"Look at George Simenon," I said. "He churned out six books a year for ten years, some in only a few weeks! I've figured it out, I'm working way below my potential."

I had done some calculations and I presented them to Rachel as follows.

"There are 168 hours in a week. You need to sleep, say, 50 hours a week. Of the remaining 118, you might spend about 20 hours a week eating, or preparing to, three times a day. That leaves 98 hours. Of these, perhaps 3 hours a day are spent in some way with loved ones; that's 21 hours a week, leaving 77 hours.

"Let's assume 8 hours a week are consumed by shopping and unforeseen distractions; allow another 4 to attend to ablutions and necessary bodily functions. Finally, then, there are 65 hours a week—almost 10 hours a day—in which to write, spit or chew gum. Even if 4 of these are spent looking at the wall or staring into space, that still leaves about 6 hours a day for actually, physically, putting down one sentence after another. Do you know how many sentences you can write in 42 hours?"

Rachel rolled her eyes and said nothing.

"I do. At an average length of 10 words, even I, a mediocre typist, can write a sentence in about 20 seconds. That's 3 a minute. In 42 hours there are 2520 minutes, enough time to write 7560 sentences—let's say 6000 even, allowing for breaks to refer to a dictionary or consult a thesaurus.

"The average typed page, double-spaced, has 28 sentences, which means that in *one week* I should be able to turn out just over 214 pages. That's a respectable book-length manuscript."

I sat back and smiled ruefully.

"Even if I spent 3 months—that's 546 hours of 6-hour writing days—polishing what I produced in a week, I figure I should be able to write 4 books a year with no sweat. In leap-years I could manage at least a few more paragraphs."

I looked at Rachel. Her head was spinning, I thought she'd turn into honey-mustard.

"What do you think of that?"

"Sounds to me like a complex," said Rachel, and threw up.

Seminar Three

Any questions from last time?

You keep referring to Jung's model of the psyche—the ego's here, there's the shadow and persona, the Self's in charge, and everywhere there's a mess of complexes. How do we know that's the way it really is?

We don't. A model is only a paradigm of how things might be. It's an idea, an image in your head, a way of looking at things to help you understand them. A model doesn't assert that something *is* so, it simply illustrates a particular mode of observation.

So what's to believe?

Well, that's a good question. Think of what we know about the material world, what we call the physical sciences—electricity, radio and tv, engineering, astronomy, building roads and bridges, sending people into space and so on. How to do all that didn't fall from the sky. It developed over a long period of time, and at every stage a lot of people were involved, experimenting with different models. Somebody had an idea of the way things are—how X affects Y, say, and what happens then to Z. When they tried it out and it didn't work, they thought of another way, a new model, and tried again. Trial and error, over and over. Whatever worked was put into use. That's the scientific method. Everything we've learned from it and put into practice—and this includes just about everything we have and use in our everyday lives—we call civilization.

Physics deals with what you can touch and build. No nonsense, you can put your finger on it. Water freezes and boils at certain temperatures and bridges buckle under just *that* much stress. We know exactly what time the sun will rise, day in and day out, and when it will set.

Psychology isn't so cut and dried, but still, anything we learn about ourselves in any systematic way depends on a model— some idea of what goes on in us, why we do what we do. Only the psyche isn't like a piece of wood, you can't put your finger on it.

Jung prided himself on being an empirical scientist. All his ideas grew out of his experience of himself and the people he worked with. It's true that some of his theories and concepts aren't provable in the way the freezing point of water is, but the individual psyche isn't amenable to test tubes or statistics.

That's not what a behavioral psychologist would say.

No, but you see they're working from a different model, a mechanistic view of the mind. They run controlled experiments on rats and guinea pigs and do statistical analyses, and believe their results apply to human beings. And some of them do! I say good luck to them, but I happen to prefer Jung's model. It leaves room for the soul.

That's why Jung's been called a mystic.

Yes, and his critics use the term pejoratively, meaning he was not scientific. But my understanding of the word "mystic" is that it refers to someone with an unusual inner vision. Jung certainly had that. The twenty volumes of his *Collected Works* reveal a man of far-reaching vision and great practical wisdom.

Jung the so-called mystic started off in psychiatry, working as an intern with schizophrenics. Then there was his seminal work on typology and his unique approach to the symbolic interpretation of dreams. His theory of archetypes and his concept of the collective unconscious is just now becoming acceptable. Jung pioneered the psychological interpretation of arcane alchemical texts and explored the mysterious connection between mind and matter, the kind of experience we call synchronistic.

Jung had an earthy appreciation of the havoc wreaked in people's lives by complexes, but he also had a spiritual side. Near the end of his life, when asked if he believed in God, Jung said, "I don't believe, I *know*." And he wasn't referring to a mindless faith but to his own experience.

I had a mystical experience once, it happened in a pub. I had a real conflict, I didn't know what to do. I was looking at the wall and sipping my beer and suddenly everything became clear . . .

I know what you mean. It's not something you can repeat, so it doesn't fall into the conventional scientific mold. But Jung's model allows for that kind of experience.

I've heard it said that Jungian psychology is about soul-making.

Yes, I wouldn't dispute that. I'm temperamentally prosaic, so I seldom think about soul from one day to the next. But when I do, the only way I can understand the progression of my life is in terms of soul. Soul happens when you ponder alone in the still of the night. Soul happens when you grapple with the meaning of your life. Soul is what you are, as opposed to what you seem to be. That's not theology, it's experiential reality.

Of course, you can only go so far with a theory, a mental model. At some point you have to look at how its application measures up to experience. That's where you and I come in. If Jung's view of the psyche doesn't accord with that of other individuals, then analytical psychology is dead as a doornail. At the moment, I'm happy to say, it's alive and kicking.

Paragraph 328 is rather long, so let's take it in sections. Here's the first part:

Unconscious motivations are of a personal and of a general nature. First of all, there are the motives deriving from parental influence. The relationship of the young man to his mother, and of the girl to her father, is the determining factor in this respect. It is the strength of the bond to the parents that unconsciously influences the choice of husband or wife, either positively or negatively. Conscious love for either parent favours the choice of a like mate, while an unconscious tie (which need not by any means express itself consciously as love) makes the choice difficult and imposes characteristic modifications. In order to understand them, one must know first of all the cause of the unconscious tie to the parents, and under what conditions it forcibly modifies, or even prevents, the conscious choice.

Jung is talking here about the influence of the parental complexes, by which he means all those emotionally charged images and ideas associated with the personal mother and father.

I still miss my mother.

I'd be happy if I never saw mine again.

As Jung says, we can be tied to the parents unconsciously whether our conscious feelings toward them are good or bad. Everything we experienced from our parents in early life is part of the content of the parental complexes. That's bound to affect our choice of a mate—it's the personal part of the unconscious motivations Jung refers to.

Now, in our last session we talked about the archetypal core of a complex. Behind the mother complex is the mother archetype, and behind the father complex is the father archetype. Jung called the combination of these two, complex and archetype together, the *parental imago*. This imago is composed of both the experience of the personal parents and collective elements already present in the psyche. It's the archetypal dimension that gives our parents a kind of magical influence over us. Even after they're gone, we still think of how they might react to what we do—like the old idea of ancestral spirits. Here's Jung:

> So long as a positive or negative resemblance to the parents is the deciding factor in a love choice, the release from the parental imago, and hence from childhood, is not complete.[40]

I married Michael because I loved him, my parents didn't even like him!

And do you know what attracted you, why you loved him?

I loved him for what he was.

What he was? I wouldn't doubt your feeling, but what exactly *was* he? Was he, is he, only what you thought he was? You have a

---

[40] "Mind and Earth," *Civilization in Transition,* CW 10, par. 74.

shadow, so does he. Do you know what it looks like? Did his shadow win your heart or did you fall in love with what you saw on the surface, his persona? I don't mean to be sarcastic, these are just rhetorical questions.

Ret . . . ?

He's thinking out loud, he doesn't expect you to answer.

Well, I want to. I knew he used dope and had other girlfriends. I suppose you'd call that shadow, but it didn't bother me. I mean it didn't used to . . .

I think this isn't the place to go into what your husband's shadow looks like, or how you feel about him now. But from everything you know about your husband, is he like your father or quite different? And then, *how* is he the same, *how* is he different?

These are the kind of questions a woman has to put to herself if she wants to understand the unconscious motivations that lead her to fall for a particular man and not someone else. It's the same for a man, only his focus would be on the resemblance between his mother and the woman he goes for.

It's not easy, this business of sorting out what's going on behind our backs, what we're unconscious of. We may think we're in charge, it feels like that, but we seldom are. Of course we usually only realize it in retrospect! That's the way it goes. Only by living out our compulsions do we get to know about them.

Why does Jung emphasize, in the choice of a mate, the influence of a man's relationship with his mother, and a woman's with her father? Why not the other way round?

That has to do with Jung's idea—and it's an important part of his model of the psyche—that a man has an unconscious feminine side, his anima, and a woman has an animus, a masculine side. What these are like, how they function in a particular case, is influenced by the parent of the opposite sex. The mother/anima colors a man's feeling life, his emotional tone, and the father/animus manifests in a woman's thoughts and ideas, the way she thinks. In both cases the influence is at work on an unconscious level, and it can be quite different from the conscious relationship with that parent.

Let's look at the next part of paragraph 328, where Jung introduces the idea of the parents' unlived life and how that affects us.

> Generally speaking, all the life which the parents could have lived, but of which they thwarted themselves for artificial motives, is passed on to the children in substitute form. That is to say, the children are driven unconsciously in a direction that is intended to compensate for everything that was left unfulfilled in the lives of their parents. Hence it is that excessively moral-minded parents have what are called "unmoral" children, or an irresponsible wastrel of a father has a son with a positively morbid amount of ambition, and so on.

Do you understand what unlived life means?

Shadow?

Yes, in general it would be all those qualities and talents and ambitions—good, bad and neutral—that are repressed or never get to see the light of day.

My mother always wanted to go on the stage.

Why didn't she?

Oh, you know, she got married and had kids . . .

Do you know what effect that had on you?

Well, I love going to plays . . .

I suppose our parents were also unconsciously compensating for their parents' unlived lives?

Certainly, on and on it goes, from one generation to the next. For instance, you might find yourself emulating the life of a great-great-grandparent, because just *that* is the unlived life your grandparent picked up from one or other of the parents and lived out, and so *your* parent didn't have to. . . . I should say I find this a much more acceptable explanation for the strange things we find ourselves doing, and for some of the images in our dreams too, than the idea of reincarnation, the notion of past lives.

My dad's a lawyer, he wished he'd been a doctor, now I'm one.

Yes, but of course we have to be careful here to differentiate between an unconscious influence and what we've been encouraged to do or be because we have a natural talent of our own.

It isn't always easy to see, compensation, but it's usually there. A man whose father was an incorrigible womanizer, a Don Juan, finds himself obsessively attached to his wife and kids, or vice versa. A woman abandoned by her mother goes into nursing, or maybe her kitchen becomes the favorite hangout for every kid on the block, that kind of thing. And then there's the tearaway son or daughter of what Jung calls here excessively moral-minded parents.

Would a woman be more likely to be affected by her mother's un-lived life than her father's?

No, I don't think so. Unlived life doesn't seem to be gender specific. You pick up on the unconscious of both parents and put it all together in quite an individual way.

What's wrong with that?

Nothing, if you know what you're doing! You see, when you're unconsciously fulfilling your parents' dreams, or maybe those of some long-gone ancestor, you miss out on your own individual destiny. You can't individuate in someone else's skin.

Individuate . . . ?

That means to become what we were meant to be. Here . . . :

> Individuation is an expression of that biological process—simple or complicated as the case may be—by which every living thing becomes what it was destined to become from the beginning.[41]

---

[41] *Psychology and Religion,* CW 11, par. 460.

What about the artificial motives Jung refers to?

I think it would be not doing something for persona reasons—what would *they* think, the neighbors, friends and so on. You wouldn't be unconsciously driven to be an artist, say, just because your father wasn't one. Maybe he had no talent or desire in that direction. Only if he'd swallowed that dream, because his family wouldn't stand for it or convinced him he'd never make a living at it, or maybe his friends thought it was a dumb idea . . .

It's what the parents *could* have lived, but didn't for the wrong reasons, that's the kind of thing that's unconsciously passed on to the next generation.

It sounds pretty complicated.

How does all this affect relationships?

Well that's a good question. One implication is that the more of our own life we can possibly live out—and let's include our secret desires here, they can be especially troublesome!—and the more conscious we become of how we came to be what we are, why we do what we do, the less likely it is that our kids will be saddled with something that isn't theirs.

I've always encouraged my son to do his best.

I dare say. But what if his idea of what's best is different from yours? And what about *being* his best? That might not fall in with your plans! Of course, now we're talking about projection again, your expectations of your son, but that too is a factor in our unlived life. How do you relate to a son or daughter who's doing—or being—what you wouldn't dare but would unconsciously like to?

Badly, I expect.

Maybe you'd try to beat it out of them.

Let's take a break.

*

We left off with the question, what does the unlived life of the parents have to do with relationships? I suggested it would affect how they relate to their children and the kind of expectations they'd have of them. And what about the effect on the children, how they grow up relating to the outside world, to other people? Do you think their parents' unlived life would only affect their choice of a profession or their morality?

Are we talking about how our parents' unlived life affected us, or the influence of our own unlived life on our kids?

Both.

There'd be a ripple affect in other areas, like, as Jung says, who we're attracted to.

We couldn't be sure of why we—or our kids—did anything!

Yes, we can get some idea of what this might look like from the next part of paragraph 328:

> The worst results flow from parents who have kept themselves arti-ficially unconscious. Take the case of a mother who deliberately keeps herself unconscious so as not to disturb the pretence of a "satisfactory" marriage. Unconsciously she will bind her son to her, more or less as a substitute for a husband. The son, if not forced di-rectly into homosexuality, is compelled to modify his choice in a way that is contrary to his true nature.

Here Jung uses the example of a woman—but it could just as well be a man—who can't or won't leave an unsatisfactory marriage. The frustration and resentment are passed on to the kids. In such a case, the unlived life of the parent would actually include having a good relationship! . . .

The mother who won't come to grips with what's going wrong between her and her husband—that's artificial unconsciousness, you see, because otherwise, if she became conscious, she might have to change her whole life—instead looks to her son for the relationship she doesn't have with her husband. I expect we'd agree this is not healthy for the son.

Couldn't she also look for it with another man?

It would take the load off the son.

If she had one.

Yes, but to have an affair I think she'd have to be more conscious of what she really wanted. It's a big step, there'd certainly be a conflict, and that's liable to lead to consciousness! The son's safer. She can at least think of herself as a faithful wife.

And the neighbors won't notice . . .

This offhand remark of Jung's, "if not forced into homosexuality," doesn't sit well with me. I don't know any mother who'd be pleased if her son were homosexual. Surely no woman would force her son to be gay! Well, I wouldn't . . .

That's just the point, you see, she's not in charge. What she wants is one thing, what she gets is something else. Jung says that the two typical effects, the extremes, of the close bond between mother and son are homosexuality and Don Juanism. Here . . . :

> In homosexuality, the son's entire heterosexuality is tied to the mother in an unconscious form; in Don Juanism, he unconsciously seeks his mother in every woman he meets.[42]

I've heard the claim that homosexuality correlates with the absence of a strong father figure in a man's early life.

Yes, no doubt that can be a causal factor. I'm more interested here in the effect. Where the man's heterosexual libido, his instinctive sexual energy, is captive to the mother, he can't muster any interest in girls, or maybe he tries but is impotent. There's a kind of secret conspiracy between mother and son. The incest taboo usually prevents this from being acted out, but the sexual urge won't be denied, and it may very

---

[42] "Psychological Aspects of the Mother Archetype," CW 9i, *The Archetypes and the Collective Unconscious,* CW 9i, par. 162.

well find an outlet with other men.

Of course the man himself might feel ashamed about this, though there's no good reason to. In such cases he's not in charge either.

Was Jung homophobic?

I wouldn't say so, we're only talking about developmental homosexuality, a neurotic distortion of what under other circumstances would be a natural, heterosexual urge. That's quite different from constitutional homosexuality, where there's an innate attraction to the same sex. Jung himself acknowledged that homosexuality isn't necessarily pathological or neurotic.[43]

A growing boy's path to mature manhood, psychologically speaking, is strewn with all kinds of obstacles. And one of the general difficulties is leaving the charmed circle of childhood, where the mother answers every call.

As a man and a single parent of a twelve-year-old boy, I don't know how to relate to that.

Yes, well . . . presumably you're doing your best to fulfil the archetypal role of mother—nourishing, protecting, all the positive aspects of the mother archetype? That would involve your feminine side, your anima. Or maybe you have a nanny . . .

No, we tried that and it didn't work.

So you're it. When I say mother, hear father.

I'm bringing up my nephew. My sister didn't want him.

When I say mother, hear aunt . . . There are lots of possible combinations. Let's agree that in this context mother is shorthand for the primary caregiver. Okay?

So, the boy grows up in a safe circle of care . . .

Well I didn't. It was one beating after another, I never felt safe.

---

43 "Concerning the Archetypes and the Anima Concept," ibid., par. 146.

Yes, that happens too, but it doesn't rule out an unconscious tie.

Look at it this way, at least you knew early on how cruel the world can be. Those of us who had positive mothering are surprised out of our boots. The world is not there for our benefit, it doesn't just fall into our lap. At some point we have to deal with ogres and dragons, so to speak—women who behave like negative mothers, men who don't care for our feelings and so on. That's the hero's journey.

When I went to the Jung Institute in Zürich, the administrative secretary was an officious woman in her sixties, short and wide. Everyone called her Frau Baba Yaga—that's the witch in Russian fairy tales who eats heroes for breakfast. If you could stand up to her, it was said, you could get through the training program. She scolded you no matter what you did. She insisted on rigorous procedures that made no sense at all and she wouldn't bend the rules an inch. And when you finally had everything in order, she'd come up with yet another obscure regulation you hadn't complied with.

She was eminently fair, of course. She treated all the trainees the same way. No matter how old they were, their education or social standing, she treated us all as naughty children.

Were you scared of her? . . .

As a matter of fact, I was terrified! It took all my courage to approach her about anything. I did it cap in hand. I knew I'd get a tongue-lashing at first, that's for sure, but if I was very lucky I might leave with a pat on the head.

The women stood up to this treatment better than the men. I don't know, maybe women just naturally find it easier to deal with a negative mother. If they've had one, it's old hat; if they haven't, they adapt more quickly. Or maybe they just know what they're capable of themselves.

My friend Arnold knew what to do. When he went to register, Frau Baba Yaga told him his name wasn't on the list, he'd have to go back to Canada and reapply. Arnold spotted his application filed under his Christian name.

"That's me," he growled, "and if you don't like it you can piss up your sleeve."

She let him in.

That's a true story?!

Honest! . . . Well, close enough . . . I learned a lot about myself through this woman, and in the end I even came to like her. My analyst helped, he gave me the right perspective. He was on the Curatorium, the governing body of the Institute. I couldn't understand why they kept her on, so one day I asked him.

"That woman is a menace," I raged, "she's quite crazy!"

My analyst shrugged. "It's not her," he said, "it's that inner man of hers, her animus. You'll have to learn to tell the difference. She herself has a kind heart. He does not. Think of her animus as the dragon that guards the treasure. A sharp tongue is like a dragon breathing fire. It's the hero's task to outwit the dragon. She's really quite useful, she separates the men from the boys."

And women . . .?

The hero's journey applies to women too, possibly through her animus. It's one of those archetypal motifs that turns up in a lot of myths and fairy tales.[44] Of course in real life the tasks for a woman are somewhat different, but Jung believed that we can't get far on this journey until we separate from the mother, our protected past— well, more or less. A man, says Jung, needs a faithless Eros. Yes, I know that sounds strange! . . .

Eros? . . .

Eros refers to our feelings and how we relate to other people. Jung associated it with the feminine principle, as the complementary opposite to masculine Logos—discrimination, structure, that sort of thing.

---

[44] See Joseph Campbell, *Hero with a Thousand Faces* (Bollingen Series XVII), Princeton: Princeton University Press, 1949, and *The Survival Papers*, pp. 77ff.

In the present context Eros means the man's primal connection with his mother. Jung says:

> [The world] makes demands on the masculinity of a man, on his ardour, above all on his courage and resolution when it comes to throwing his whole being into the scales. For this he would need a faithless Eros, one capable of forgetting his mother and undergoing the pain of relinquishing the first love of his life.[45]

And then he pinpoints the mother's unconscious hold:

> The mother, foreseeing this danger, has carefully inculcated into him the virtues of faithfulness, devotion, loyalty, so as to protect him from the moral disruption which is the risk of every life adventure. He has learnt these lessons only too well, and remains true to his mother.[46]

And here's the possible result, right back to the homosexual issue:

> This naturally causes her the deepest anxiety (when, to her greater glory, he turns out to be a homosexual, for example) and at the same time affords her an unconscious satisfaction that is positively mythological. For, in the relationship now reigning between them, there is consummated the immemorial and most sacred archetype of the marriage of mother and son. What, after all, has commonplace reality to offer, with its registry offices, pay envelopes, and monthly rent, that could outweigh the mystic awe of the *hieros gamos?*[47]

I should say, too, that a father who's afraid of his homoerotic shadow, his attraction to other men, can also be instrumental in his son's unconscious movement in that direction.

Unlived life.

Yes, I know a man who's a real jock, he's what you'd call a man's man. As it happens, his brother is homosexual. My straight friend has done all the traditional macho things with his son—camping, hunting, hockey and so on. His son is fourteen, he just likes to read

---

[45] "The Syzygy: Anima and Animus," *Aion,* CW 9ii, par. 22.
[46] Ibid.
[47] Ibid.

and listen to Mozart, he's not interested in girls. He loves his uncle though!

As you can see, everything we're talking about has to do with un-lived life, at least psychically.

I've heard it said that Jung lived out everything but stupidity, and his son's doing that!

Yes, I've heard that story too and I suspect it's apocryphal.

Apock . . . ?

There's no truth to it.

Continuing with paragraph 328, and still referring to the mother's influence, Jung goes on to suggest some possibilities other than ho-mosexuality, other ways in which a man's choice of a mate might be unconsciously modified:

> He may, for instance, marry a girl who is obviously inferior to his mother and therefore unable to compete with her; or he will fall for a woman of a tyrannical and overbearing disposition, who may per-haps succeed in tearing him away from his mother. The choice of a mate, if the instincts have not been vitiated, may remain free from these influences, but sooner or later they will make themselves felt as obstacles.

From bad to worse!

What's vishiated mean?

And all that's the result of the mother not leaving a bad marriage?

Only if her motives for staying are unconscious. Whether she leaves or not is usually a practical question. The psychologically important point is *why* she does one or the other, and how conscious she is of what she does. Vitiated here means impaired—if the instincts aren't fundamentally impaired, the son will initially choose freely, or seem to, and only later experience the effects of the mother-bond.

How much later?

Well, there's no telling with any accuracy. In general, I'd say about midlife—anywhere from, say, thirty-five to sixty. . . . That's typically the period when we wake up, if we ever do, to what we are, what we've become compared to what we once wanted to be.

In early life we tend to just forge ahead, get on with it, we aren't generally inclined to be psychological about what happens to us along the way. In the second half of life, when we've made our mark, or maybe realize we've missed it, we're more apt to look back on our lives and question what was going on. We don't always like what we see, and for a man the obstacles to change, according to Jung, are rooted back in that idyllic bond between mother and son, the protected space he grew up in . . . well, many of us did.

This is beginning to sound like Freud. Everything's reduced to sex and early childhood. We're just victims of our past.

I don't see it like that, and Jung didn't either. When you look into it, the difference between the two is quite pronounced. Jung interpreted libido very broadly, as psychic energy in general, not just sexual. And whereas Freud sought a cure in understanding the cause, the original source of a psychological problem, Jung's view was that the difficulties we run into in the present also have a meaning for the future—when the time is ripe, the psyche prods us to move on.

Jung wrote a book about this, *Symbols of Transformation.* I'll read you just a brief passage, to give you an idea of where he stands. Here he's talking particularly about a young man on the brink of life, struggling to leave the nest, but the same psychological issues can turn up at any age:

> The forward-striving libido which rules the conscious mind of the son demands separation from the mother, but his childish longing for her prevents this by setting up a psychic resistance that manifests itself in all kinds of neurotic fears—that is to say, in a general fear of life. The more a person shrinks from adapting himself to reality, the greater becomes the fear which increasingly besets his path . . . . The reasons for this are generally projected outside oneself: the fault lies with external circumstances, or else the parents are made respon-

sible. And indeed, it remains to be found out how much the mother is to blame for not letting the son go. The son will naturally try to explain everything by the wrong attitude of the mother, but he would do better to refrain from all such futile attempts to excuse his own ineptitude by laying the blame on his parents.[48]

Do you see? Jung didn't say we shouldn't try to understand the past, only that we can't hide behind it. At some point we ourselves have to accept responsibility for what's happening *now* in our lives, and then take charge of what comes next.

I appreciate all this talk about mother and son, I really do. But I have problems with two girls. Did Jung have anything to say about the relationship between mother and daughter?

Yes, he certainly did, and considerably more than about fathers and daughters or fathers and sons. Of course some of his ideas are outdated, and since he's not a woman they come from the outside, they have to be taken *cum grano salis,* as Jung would say.

With a grain of salt.

Never mind, I'd like to hear.

Me too.

Sure, my wife would be interested. We have a ten-year-old girl.

All in favor? Okay, I don't mind.

Most of Jung's views on the subject of mothers and daughters are found in a lecture he gave in 1938, called "Psychological Aspects of the Mother Complex."[49] First there are some general observations on the mother archetype, and then he discusses the different qualities, some positive and others negative, that have been associated with mother down through the ages, the kind of images and symbolic associations we meet in literature, mythology, folklore and so on.

---

[48] "The Battle for Deliverance from the Mother," *Symbols of Transformation,* CW 5, par. 456.

[49] *The Archetypes and the Collective Unconscious,* CW 9i.

These images of mother are in our blood, and we're always prone to project them onto an actual woman.

The most convenient hook for these projections is usually the personal mother. The archetypal element gives her a particular authority and numinosity, a larger-than-life quality, and that's what forms the foundation for the individual mother complex.

According to Jung, the possible effects of the mother complex on the daughter range from an exaggeration of the feminine instincts to their inhibition. In the first case, there's an intensification of the maternal instinct. Her primary goal, often her only one, is childbirth. All she wants is to have kids.

What would such a woman's relationships look like?

The mother's or the daughter's?

Either/or, both/and. Women are daughters and daughters grow up to be mothers who have daughters . . .

She'd be overprotective.

She'd probably mother the men in her life.

Yes, Jung goes rather further than that. He says:

> To her the husband is . . . of secondary importance; he is first and foremost the instrument of procreation, and she regards him merely as an object to be looked after, along with children, poor relations, cats, dogs, and household furniture.[50]

And she's right! . . .

Jung also says this kind of woman tends to be unconscious of her own personality. She appears to be selfless and she identifies with those she takes care of. That would mean she'd live her life in and through others. Listen to this:

> First she gives birth to the children, and from then on she clings to them, for without them she has no existence whatsoever. Like

---

[50] Ibid., par. 167.

Demeter, she compels the gods by her stubborn persistence to grant her the right of possession over her daughter. Her Eros develops exclusively as a maternal relationship while remaining unconscious as a personal one.[51]

Sounds like power to me.

To Jung too! He goes on:

An unconscious Eros always expresses itself as will to power. Women of this type, though continually "living for others," are, as a matter of fact, unable to make any real sacrifice. Driven by ruthless will to power and a fanatical insistence on their own maternal rights, they often succeed in annihilating not only their own personality but also the personal lives of their children.[52]

That's my mother to a tee! She was always in charge, even my dad wouldn't cross her . . .

Now, the second possibility when the mother's maternal side is overemphasized is that the daughter's own mothering instincts can be inhibited or even wiped out. Then the result is an overdeveloped and overpersonalized Eros. Jung says this invariably leads to an unconscious incestuous relationship with the father and therefore, quite naturally, to jealousy of the mother . . .[53]

This kind of woman has no desire for children of her own. Her focus is on romantic adventures, the more intense the better. I'm afraid Jung gives her rather short shrift:

A woman of this type loves romantic and sensational episodes for their own sake, and is interested in married men, less for themselves than for the fact that they are married and so give her an opportunity to wreck a marriage, that being the whole point of her manoeuvre.

---

[51] Ibid.

[52] Ibid. See also *Two Essays on Analytical Psychology*, CW 7, par. 78: "Where love reigns, there is no will to power; and where the will to power is paramount, love is lacking."

[53] Jung points out that the projection of the father's anima can also play a significant role in this domestic drama. ("Psychological Aspects of the Mother Complex," *The Archetypes and the Collective Unconscious*, CW 9i, par. 168, note 6)

Once the goal is attained, her interest evaporates for lack of any maternal instinct, and then it will be someone else's turn. This type is noted for its remarkable unconsciousness.[54]

I've been burned by those pixies more than once!

Cheaters never prosper . . .

Jung says her fate is to be a disturbing element in other people's relationships, but this needn't be seen as entirely destructive. He quotes these lines from Goethe's *Faust*—

> Part of that power which would
> Ever work evil but engenders good,[55]

—suggesting that the conflict she stirs up can actually be healthy for all concerned, and not least for herself. Remember, one of Jung's basic ideas is that conflict is a stimulus to consciousness.[56]

It all sounds pretty extreme.

Yes, Jung had a habit of speaking hyperbolically, to make a point.

Hyper . . . ?

He liked to exaggerate.

Thank you. Now, Jung goes on to describe a third type of woman, another possible result when the mother is caught up in . . . well, being a mother. The daughter might identify with her mother and then be unconscious of both her own maternal instinct and her own Eros. It would all be projected onto the mother.

> Everything which reminds her [the daughter] of motherhood, responsibility, personal relationships, and erotic demands arouses feelings of inferiority and compels her to run away—to her mother, naturally,

---

54 Ibid., par. 168.

55 Ibid., par. 181 (from *Faust,* part 1, act 1).

56 "The stirring up of conflict is a Luciferian virtue in the true sense of the word. Conflict engenders fire, the fire of affects and emotions, and like every other fire it has two aspects, that of combustion and that of creating light." (Ibid., par. 179)

who lives to perfection everything that seems unattainable to her daughter. As a sort of superwoman (admired involuntarily by the daughter), the mother lives out for her beforehand all that the girl might have lived for herself. She is content to cling to her mother in selfless devotion, while at the same time unconsciously striving, almost against her will, to tyrannize over her, naturally under the mask of complete loyalty and devotion. The daughter leads a shadow-existence, often visibly sucked dry by her mother, and she prolongs her mother's life by a sort of continuous blood transfusion.[57]

As you see, there'd be a strong tie to the mother, while unconsciously the daughter would yearn to be free. And there's a good possibility she'd feel her mother was holding her back. You can imagine the tension between them.

My poor baby . . .

I'd hate to meet her on a starry night!

You'd be surprised. These women are particularly good hooks for men's anima projections. They can seem to be anything you want. And we're suckers for that! Well, I know I am, I've been attracted to more than one. Jung expresses it like this:

Despite their shadowiness and passivity, they command a high price on the marriage market. First, they are so empty that a man is free to impute to them anything he fancies. In addition, they are so unconscious that the unconscious puts out countless invisible feelers, veritable octopus-tentacles, that suck up all masculine projections; and this pleases men enormously. All that feminine indefiniteness is the longed-for counterpart of male decisiveness and single-mindedness, which can be satisfactorily achieved only if a man can get rid of everything doubtful, ambiguous, vague, and muddled by projecting it upon some charming example of feminine innocence.[58]

Jung adds a footnote here:

This type of woman has an oddly disarming effect on her husband,

---

[57] Ibid., par. 169.

[58] Ibid. See also M. Esther Harding, *The Way of All Women* (New York: Harper Colophon, 1975), especially chapter 1, "All Things to All Men."

but only until he discovers that the person he has married and who shares his nuptial bed is his mother-in-law.[59]

I know just what he means!

Of course it needn't turn out so badly. These women often become devoted and self-sacrificing mates. That's because even if they can get quit of their mother, they're liable to project their talents, their own unconscious gifts, onto their partner. And then, says Jung,

> We have the spectacle of a totally insignificant man who seemed to have no chance whatsoever suddenly soaring as if on a magic carpet to the highest summits of achievement. *Cherchez la femme,* and you have the secret of his success. These women remind me . . . of hefty great bitches who turn tail before the smallest cur simply because he is a terrible male and it never occurs to them to bite him.[60]

I get the impression Jung was a misogynist. These wet dishrags, is that all he saw? Did he ever say anything good about women, I mean really complimentary?

Yes, but wait, you haven't heard the worst!

In Jung's view, the three types we've been talking about are linked together by a lot of intermediate stages. The most important of these is where there's an overwhelming resistance to the mother and everything she stands for. This is your real dragon lady, a man's worst nightmare—well, mine! Jung calls her the supreme example of the negative mother complex.

> The motto of this type is: Anything, so long as it is not like Mother! . . . This kind of daughter knows what she does *not* want, but is usually completely at sea as to what she would choose as her own fate. . . . Should she get as far as marrying, either the marriage will be used for the sole purpose of escaping from her mother, or else a diabolical fate will present her with a husband who shares all the essential traits of her mother's character. All instinctive processes meet with unexpected difficulties; either sexuality does not

---

[59] "Psychological Aspects of the Mother Archetype," *The Archetypes and the Collective Unconscious,* CW 9i, par. 169.
[60] Ibid., par. 182.

function properly, or the children are unwanted, or maternal duties seem unbearable, or the demands of marital life are responded to with impatience and irritation. . . . Resistance to the mother as *uterus* often manifests itself in menstrual disturbances, failure of conception, abhorrence of pregnancy, hemorrhages and excessive vomiting during pregnancy, miscarriages, and so on. The mother as *materia,* "matter," may be at the back of these women's impatience with objects, their clumsy handling of tools and crockery and bad taste in clothes.[61]

God! I'm tearing my hair!

I know women who'd hang him in effigy for that . . .

You understand, I'm not here to defend Jung's views, I'm just the messenger. You can take them for what they're worth. Some of the things he says about women are strange to me too. That's why I wonder about his personal relationships. Some of them must have been pretty disappointing!

At the same time, I can relate his descriptions to a lot of women I've known myself. And what he says about them has also given me a handle on my own emotional life. I thank him for that.

---

[61] Ibid., par. 170.

Interlude

"I'm puzzled," said Rachel. She was huddled on the sofa with that paisley scarf I brought her back from Harrod's, the one with all the eyes and feathers on it.

"Yes?" As if I didn't know.

"Well, this isn't quite what I expected."

I played dumb.

"You started off with Jung's essay on marriage, but you've only gone through a few paragraphs, and marriage hardly comes into it."

"The seminar, this book, isn't about marriage," I said, "it's about the psychology involved in an intimate relationship."

Rachel crossed her arms, not a good sign. "It's hard to see what some of it has to do with any relationship at all."

I considered my response. I live alone, but not in isolation. I get ideas and some of them are inspired by Rachel, but what comes next is up to me. I get caught up in thoughts, Rachel knows how she feels. We work together, but it's a fluid thing.

"The point of all this," I said, "is that the possibility of having a psychological relationship hinges on an understanding of oneself. That's the bottom line. It's the 'you' in the title and the 'inside out' in the subtitle. It's also the essential meaning of Jung's opening statement: 'Whenever we speak about a psychological relationship we presuppose one that is conscious.' You can't understand the implications of that without having a pretty good idea of what's involved in being conscious. And for that you need to know about complexes, projections and so on."

"Yes, I see all that." Rachel frowned. "But then why choose this essay?"

"Because it's the only place Jung presents the metaphor of the container and the contained. That's what we're working up to. And as I said at the start, it leads to a consideration of just about every basic principle of Jung's."

77

"You did that in your *Lexicon* and *Types.*"[62]

"Well . . . there are midlife issues I want to deal with."

"You did that in *The Survival Papers.*"

"Not in the same way."

"As far as I can see, you're repeating yourself."

I winced. It was true, I had nothing new to say.

"Yes," I said, "but of those out there who might benefit from Jungian psychology, how many would pick up a dictionary on the subject? There are a lot of people hurting because they have no psychological perspective. They might read a book about midlife crisis, but what if they don't know that's what they've got?"

"So what's different about this?"

"The hook, the package . . . Oh, and in case you didn't notice, we're not just talking about relationship, we're having one."

Rachel looked doubtful.

"The world is not waiting breathless for another book by you."

That hurt. I pretended it didn't.

"Think of what it means to the environment," said Rachel. "How many trees are you killing?"

I rose to this.

"Trees? Trees? I love trees! Second only to elephants. How many do you think will be left if people don't become conscious? I'm not an extravert, I won't march in the streets to preserve the rain-forest. What I *can* do, in my own way, is speak to the source, the individual. Jung said the most important thing was to educate the educators.[63] And that's where I stand."

Rachel gave me a big hug.

"I like that," she said, unbuttoning her blouse. "I like it when you know what you're doing."

---

[62] *Jung Lexicon: A Primer of Terms & Concepts* (Inner City Books, 1990); *Personality Types: Jung's Model of Typology* (Inner City Books, 1987).

[63] See, for instance, "Child Development and Education," *The Development of Personality,* CW 17, pars. 108ff.

Seminar Four

The next couple of paragraphs in Jung's essay, 329 and 330, don't add much to the issues we've already talked about—unconscious identity and the influence of the parental complexes. But there are a few items worth discussing. Yes?

You didn't get to tell us the nice things Jung said about women.

Well, Jung didn't sing the praises of women per se, but his views have had a lot to do with the resurrection of the feminine principle in contemporary consciousness, bringing it out of the closet, so to speak.[64] Maybe his most significant contribution in this area was to pinpoint the feminine as the needed balance in a world that functions mostly according to traditional masculine values. And in that sense he's antipatriarchal.

Go to the index of Jung's *Collected Works*. Look under "feminine" and "anima." You'll find a wealth of references.

You said some of his ideas about women are outdated.

Yes, but only because social realities have changed. The psyche is essentially conservative, you see, it goes on in the same old way no matter what you believe.

When you've read what Jung actually wrote, you can decide for yourself whether his views are still relevant or not. Personally, I think they just aren't understood. If anything, I'd say they're about fifty years ahead of their time. Jung's concept of the anima, for instance, is difficult to follow if you don't know the age-old association

---

[64] See, for instance, Marion Woodman, "Rediscovery of the Feminine," *The Owl Was a Baker's Daughter: Obesity, Anorexia Nervosa and the Repressed Feminine* (Toronto: Inner City Books, 1980), pp. 102ff; Sylvia Brinton Perera, *Descent to the Goddess: A Way of Initiation for Women* (Toronto: Inner City Books, 1981); and *The Sacred Prostitute: Eternal Aspect of the Feminine* (Toronto: Inner City Books, 1987.

of Eros with the feminine. And without a good understanding of how these are intertwined, you can't really appreciate how they apply to individual women or, indeed, their fundamental importance in terms of a psychological relationship.

I'd like to hear what Jung said.

Me too.

Well, to be fair, we'll have to speak of both feminine *and* masculine. In Jung's model, these are working principles based on archetypal realities. They represent opposite kinds of energy. Like any pair of opposites, they aren't hostile but complementary. Opposites are only hostile when one has the upper hand or tries to lord it over the other. That's when the other side will clamor for attention.

It's the old principle of enantiodromia, which Jung defined as the emergence or activation of the unconscious opposite in the course of time.[65] Like Paul's conversion on the road to Damascus.

That misogynist!

The current interest in ancient mother goddesses after centuries of ignoring them is another example.

Are masculine and feminine associated with gender?

Not as abstract principles, but culturally, especially in the West, they usually are.

Jung didn't invent these categories, masculine and feminine, but he accepted that the qualities always and everywhere associated with them had an archetypal foundation. That's why archetypes are archetypes—they reflect the accumulated experience of the human race. All Jung did was to compare the *consensus gentium* with his own experience of men and women, and then incorporate what fit into his psychological model.

Consensus . . . ?

---

[65] See Jung, "Definitions," *Psychological Types,* CW 6, par. 709.

What people everywhere have always believed.

In Jung's earlier writings, he intuitively equated masculine consciousness with the traditional concept of Logos and feminine consciousness with that of Eros. Here is what he wrote:

> By Logos I meant discrimination, judgment, insight, and by Eros I meant the capacity to relate. I regarded both concepts as intuitive ideas which cannot be defined accurately or exhaustively. From the scientific point of view this is regrettable, but from a practical one it has its value, since the two concepts mark out a field of experience which it is equally difficult to define.[66]

Of course, in terms of individual psychology, Jung acknowledged that either Eros or Logos could be dominant in any particular man or woman. You get men who can't discriminate worth a damn and their judgment's not so good, but they relate well, you feel good when you're with them. I know men like this who are excellent day-care workers and some who are therapists. And then you find women who maybe bungle their relationships but score high in the Logos area. You find a lot of them in the professions or running their own business. They can be very efficient and competent.

Jung suggested that a reversal of type, so to speak, was due to the influence of the contrasexual archetype, the anima or animus. Like any other complex, they're always more or less unconscious.

Did Jung actually believe that a man's most natural way of functioning was through Logos?

Yes, that's the archetypal truth, if you like. A man needn't be *good* at it, it's just his natural biological bent.

And if he doesn't function in that way?

Well, theoretically it would be because his ideas and behavior patterns were overly influenced by his feminine side, his anima.

---

[66] "The Personification of the Opposites," *Mysterium Coniunctionis,* CW 14, par. 224.

That would be anima possession?

In the extreme, yes. She'd rule the roost. The man would be unconsciously identified with his emotions.

He'd be a wimp.

As a matter of fact, he might very well be a jock. Whatever, typically he'd be irritable, moody and oversensitive.

Now, for a woman—according to Jung—her conscious way of functioning, archetypally grounded in the principle of Eros, is colored by the unconscious influence of her animus. And if she were dominated by the animus—that would mean she'd lost touch with her feminine side, we'd call her animus possessed. You'd get the feeling you were dealing with a hard-hearted man.

A ball-breaker.

Well, that's the way a man might experience her. Maybe she'd just have more balls than he did.

Wouldn't his mother complex play a part?

Yes, it certainly would! A man's reactions to a woman always involve his mother complex, just as a woman's response to a man is more or less determined by her father complex.

In his later writing on alchemy, Jung described Logos and Eros as psychologically equivalent to solar and lunar consciousness, archetypal ideas analogous to the Eastern concepts of yang and yin—again, opposite but complementary kinds of energy—where yang, the masculine, is associated with *doing*—penetrating, incisive action—and yin, the feminine, with *being*—everything we think of as passive and receptive.[67] This didn't change Jung's view that Eros was more specific, meaning more natural, to feminine consciousness and Logos to masculine. And so he still attributed Eros in a man to

---

[67] See Richard Wilhelm, trans., *The I Ching or Book of Changes* (London: Routledge and Kegan Paul, 1968), Hexagrams 1 and 2.

the influence of the anima, and Logos in a woman to that of the animus. He expressed it like this:

> In a man it is the lunar anima, in a woman the solar animus, that influences consciousness in the highest degree. Even if a man is often unaware of his own anima-possession, he has, understandably enough, all the more vivid an impression of the animus-possession of his wife, and vice versa.[68]

I've read ahead. In paragraph 338 Jung says women have no soul. I mean really!

Well, he didn't mean that in a theological sense. It's not a put-down of women, it's simply a consequence of his psychological model. A man's archetypal predisposition is to function out of his head. In compensation, his unconscious has a feminine character, personified as the anima. In this sense, a woman, on the conscious level, is *all* soul. This is compensated by a masculine mind, the animus, in the unconscious.

I do get the impression that Jung was patriarchal at heart, well, at least a traditionalist. Men are like this, women are like that. There's nothing to be done about it, that's just the way it is.

That's not my reading of Jung. I think he saw enormous possibilities for change, but it depended on a man having a relationship with his inner feminine and a woman with her inner masculine. Until we make contact with these contrasexual opposites in ourselves, we're bound to continue projecting them onto those we're close to. The process of focusing on the inner axis invariably takes some weight off real-life relationships. We don't expect so much of others when we're busy getting to know ourselves . . .

An interesting implication of Jung's model—and this applies whether or not we're in touch with our inner man or woman—is that in any relationship there are at least four personalities involved. That's the psychological reality. In terms of communication between

---

68 Ibid., par. 225.

the sexes, the possibilities are quite bewildering. You can connect ego to ego, or anima to animus, or maybe the relationship is a cross-current, so to speak, between the woman's animus and the man's ego or the man's anima and the woman's ego . . .

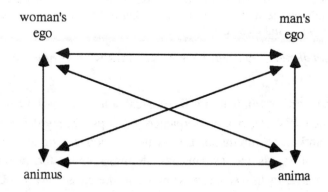

woman's ego | man's ego

animus | anima

I'd like to move on now. There's more to be said about all this, but I expect we'll come back to it.

In paragraphs 329 and 330, Jung acknowledges that the instinctive choice of a mate is all very well in terms of maintaining the human species, but again emphasizes the fact that the relationship between the two parties will be impersonal rather than psychological. In the flush of passion, says Jung, we imagine that the other is just like us, we dissolve into the other person—"one heart and one soul"—a state of complete harmony. It feels good because it's like a return to childhood, which Jung describes in paragraph 330 as "that original condition of unconscious oneness."

I imagine most of us have had an experience like that. I know I have, more than once, and I certainly don't regret it. But there's a price to pay:

> Unconsciousness results in non-differentiation, or unconscious identity. . . . It is, in truth, a genuine and incontestable experience of the Divine, whose transcendent force obliterates and consumes everything individual; a real communion with life and the impersonal power of fate. The individual will for self-possession is broken: the

woman becomes the mother, the man the father, and thus both are robbed of their freedom and made instruments of the life urge.

People in this situation, says Jung, have a relationship "wholly regulated by traditional customs and prejudices, the prototype of every conventional marriage." (par. 329)

We all know what this looks like. If we haven't experienced it ourselves, we've seen it in our parents. Mom and Pop—that's the way we see them, and more often than not it's the way they see themselves.

What's wrong with that? It's what they are!

No, it's just what they seem to be. What they are is something else. Until they know the difference there's no possibility of a psychological relationship. And the same goes for us.

I have a real cozy relationship with my husband. I like it.

Well, I'm not here to disturb that. But maybe you are! Listen to what Jung says in paragraph 331:

> Here the relationship remains within the bounds of the biological instinctive goal, the preservation of the species. Since this goal is of a collective nature, the psychological link between husband and wife will also be essentially collective, and cannot be regarded as an individual relationship in the psychological sense. We can only speak of this when the nature of the unconscious motivations has been recognized and the original identity broken down. Seldom or never does a marriage develop into an individual relationship smoothly and without crises. There is no birth of consciousness without pain.

What Jung here calls an individual relationship is of course synonomous with a psychological one. And the movement from an impersonal, instinctive relationship to one that's conscious—with at least the potential to become a bona fide *psychological* relationship—is, says Jung, virtually always accompanied by pain.

What is he referring to here and why would it be painful?

Does he mean the realization that the two are different? Separating from that original state of oneness?

The pain would be a consequence of withdrawing projections.

Yes, it would be like being wrenched anew from the womb, being thrown out of Paradise. The Christian myth of Adam and Eve is a paradigm for that. As long as Adam and Eve lived in the Garden they were happy. Happy, but unconscious. Listen to the crafty snake— that's comparable to getting a message from the unconscious—and immediately you're in trouble. Your whole world can turn upside down. You go to bed in the lap of the gods and you wake up living east of Eden . . .

What kind of message are you talking about?

Well . . . falling in love with someone new, a powerful dream, an illness or an accident of some kind. . . . The unconscious speaks in different ways. Of course some people never hear it, or pretend not to. They stay unconscious, though not necessarily happy.

Jung was fond of referring to a precept in alchemy, called the Axiom of Maria, as a metaphor for the psychological movement out of the paradisiacal state. It goes like this: "One becomes two, two becomes three, and out of the third comes the One as the fourth."[69]

One is the original state of unconscious wholeness; *two* signifies the conflict between opposites; *three* points to a potential resolution; and *the one as the fourth* is a transformed state of consciousness, relatively whole and at peace.

The Axiom of Maria is shorthand, you see, for what's involved psychologically in the process of individuation, becoming what you were meant to be. Leaving Eden is a crucial part of it. That's the beginning of consciousness, and it always involves coming to terms with opposites. Here's a neat observation by Jung:

> The conscious mind is on top, the shadow underneath, and just as high always longs for low and hot for cold, so all consciousness, perhaps without being aware of it, seeks its unconscious opposite,

---

[69] See, for instance, *Psychology and Alchemy,* CW 12, par. 209.

lacking which it is doomed to stagnation, congestion, and ossification. Life is born only of the spark of opposites.[70]

Maybe you weren't meant to leave the Garden.

Yes, that's possible, at least theoretically. Then you wouldn't get the call to move from one to two. But you see, two symbolizes any conflict situation, and that's arguably part of the human condition. Do you know anyone who has no conflicts? I don't. The major difficulties in life, in my experience, crop up in moving from two to three, and then on to four; that is, resolving conflicts and then getting back to a state of harmony within yourself—a *conscious* state of oneness. In this model, the only difference between beginning and end is the degree of consciousness.

Let's look a little closer at this remark of Jung's: "Seldom or never does a marriage develop into an individual relationship smoothly and without crises." There's a litany of possibilities behind that sentence. Withdrawing projections certainly gives rise to a fair number of crises. Another big factor is that the symbiotic bond that commonly ties lovers together can lead to a lot of animosity when the time comes to break it.

The end of togetherness.

Yes, but that's not bad, at least not in terms of becoming conscious. Togetherness is an ideal based on the archetypal motif of wholeness. Find your soul-mate and you'll live happily ever after. It's a very old idea. You find it in Greek philosophy, for instance in Plato's *Symposium,* where Aristophanes pictures humans as originally whole but arrogant. As punishment, Zeus cut them in half, and now we forever seek to replace our lost other.[71] But the fact is, even if you find him or her, you're just back to the *one* in the Axiom of Maria—a return to the Garden.

I kind of like that idea—me and my wife, working as a team.

---

[70] *Two Essays on Analytical Psychology,* CW 7, par. 78.
[71] Plato, *The Symposium,* (London: Penguin Books, 1952).

Yes, don't we all?! That's why it's an archetypal motif. But bring it down to earth, look at what's workable on an individual level compared to what's archetypally ideal. I think what Jung said is true, that you can't individuate on Mount Everest—that is, without relationships—but individuation, finding your own unique path, isn't compatible with togetherness.

Do you know that old popular song, "I Want To Be Happy, But I Can't Be Happy, Till I Make You Happy too"? That's togetherness. It's sentimental and denies the independence of both.

You see, individuation requires a focus on the inner axis, ego to unconscious, getting to know yourself. The ideal of togetherness doesn't acknowledge the natural boundaries between people, and takes no account of differences. All you're left with is unconscious identity. Individuation enables you to relate to others from a position of personal integrity. It's the basis for intimacy with distance.

That sounds so cold.

I'll grant you it's not as cozy as togetherness, but it's not as sticky either. Intimacy with distance can be as warm as you want, and it's psychologically clean. Togetherness is simply fusion with another, the submersion of two individualities into one. That's symbiosis. It can feel good for a while but psychologically it's not viable.

I don't understand.

Well, symbiosis is two hearts as one. It's what normally happens between mother and child, and that's okay, it's a good base for the child's future. It's a different story between grown-ups, where that degree of interdependence is just asking for trouble.

Jung gives an example in terms of introversion and extraversion. Where one of these two attitude-types is dominant, the other, being unconscious, is automatically projected onto another person, so it's quite usual for an introvert to fall in love with an extravert, and vice versa. As Jung says:

> Either type has a predilection to marry its opposite, each being unconsciously complementary to the other. . . . The two types there-

fore seem created for a symbiosis. The one takes care of reflection and the other sees to the initiative and practical action. When the two types marry they may effect an ideal union. So long as they are fully occupied with their adaptation to the manifold external needs of life they fit together admirably.[72]

The "external needs of life" would include those things Jung referred to in the very first paragraph of this essay, you remember, as "objective factors"—making a living, establishing a home, raising the kids and so on. When you have a job and a family there's not much time for anything else. So problems in a symbiotic relationship typically surface only later in life, when these outer challenges have been dealt with. Then, says Jung, the partners may suddenly realize they have little in common.

Hitherto they stood back to back and defended themselves against necessity. But now they turn face to face and look for understanding— only to discover that they have never understood one another. Each speaks a different language. Then the conflict between the two types begins. This struggle is envenomed, brutal, full of mutual depreciation, even when conducted quietly and in the greatest intimacy. For the value of the one is the negation of value for the other.[73]

Is that inevitable? I mean, you read about couples who've been happily married, no problems, for seventy years . . . As far as I know, my own parents were like that.

I wouldn't say it was impossible, but I'm skeptical, especially about what I read in the papers. As we've discussed, people can get pretty attached to an image of themselves as a happy couple. If two people in a close relationship never have any problems, it's usually because they hide their true feelings. On the other hand, if they're prepared to work on the relationship—accept their differences, take back the projections and so on—yes, given all that, it's possible to escape the kind of bitter struggle Jung describes.

---

72 "The Problem of the Attitude-Type," *Two Essays on Analytical Psychology,* CW 7, par. 80.
73 Ibid.

Mind you, I think that along the way they would have to leave behind popular ideas of what's involved in being happy. They'd have to define happiness in their own terms, what works for them. And in terms of a relationship, they'd have to come to a place where they could say to the other, "I love you as you are." Not for what you give me, not for what I want you to be or wish you were, but *as you are.* If you can get to that point, I think you'd have what could fairly be called a psychological relationship. Anything else is not love but power.

I love my guy for what he is, but I'd like him better if he was just a little bit different . . .

Loving someone as they are means taking the chaff with the wheat. No half-measures, no hedging your bets.

How do you work on a relationship?

Well, not by confrontation and not by discussing what's going on between you in psychological terms. Far from it! Especially not when there's ill feeling in the air. It's enough to acknowledge you're in a bad mood. I think the worst thing you can do is to talk about anima and animus and complexes and so on. Keep all that to yourself. It can help you get your own bearings, but it's just as likely to drive your partner into a frenzy. Relationships thrive on feeling values, not on what's written in books.

My idea of working on a relationship is to shut your mouth when you're ready to explode. Don't inflict your emotional reaction on the other person. Leave the room, go to your own quiet space and tear your hair out. Instead of accusing the other person of driving you crazy, say to yourself, "I feel I'm being driven crazy. Now where, in me, is that coming from?"

Ask yourself—not your partner—what complex in you has been activated, and to what purpose. The proper question is not, "Why are you doing this to me?" or "Who do you think you are?" but rather, "Why am I reacting in this way?—Who do *I* think *they* are?" That leads to the really important question: "What does this say about my psychology?" When you have a handle on that, you can go the extra step and ask, "What can I do about it?"

In that way, you establish a container, a temenos.

Temenos?

That's what the Greeks called a sacred space. Psychologically it refers to personal boundaries, a place where the gods—the complexes—can safely play. When you have a container for what's going on in you, you're less likely to contaminate your surroundings by acting out your emotions.

Aren't we allowed to get mad?

Allowed? That's not the way it works. We *do* get mad, and sometimes we have to express it because there's genuine feeling mixed in with the complex. Feeling is one of the compass points in Jung's model of typology. As a psychological function, feeling tells you what something's worth to you. There's a fine line between feeling in this sense and the emotion of the complex, and that's another value in having a container. There's a better chance you can tell the difference if you have something to slosh things around in. And then you can speak from the heart.

On the whole, you work on a relationship by keeping your mood to yourself and examining it. You don't bottle up the emotion but you also don't allow it to poison the relationship. The merit in this way of dealing with emotional reactions is that it forces us to become aware of our experience of ourselves.

You see, at some point we have to realize that we can't change the other person. But with a personal container we can change ourselves and our reactions.

What about letting it all hang out?

Yes, I remember when that was fashionable. Just blow up and speak your mind! That's what's called catharsis. There's something to be said for it, but not much. The big question is, whose mind are you speaking? Are you merely letting the complex take over? You don't know until you get some distance from the emotion, objectify it, take a stand toward it. You can't do this if you identify with it.

When you can tell the difference between yourself and the mood you're in, that's the time to speak.

I'm confused. You seem to be saying that you work on a relationship by working on yourself.

Yes, I am. The endless blather between two complexed people is a waste of time. It's just window dressing for what's going on unconsciously. It solves nothing and often makes the situation worse. This is a matter of general experience. Speaking of what happens between a man and a woman, Jung puts it quite graphically:

> When animus and anima meet, the animus draws his sword of power and the anima ejects her poison of illusion and seduction.[74]

Aren't they just as likely to fall in love?

Yes, but as Jung points out:

> The language of love is of astonishing uniformity, using the well-worn formulas with the utmost devotion and fidelity, so that once again the two partners find themselves in a banal collective situation. Yet they live in the illusion that they are related to one another in a most individual way.[75]

Don't we need some illusions in order to keep going? That's what Aldous Huxley said.

I don't know, maybe it depends on how conscious you are or want to be. I suppose there's nothing wrong with illusions as long as they don't get in the way of what's actually happening in your life.

Or vice versa.

Yes. Let's take a break.

*

---

[74] *Aion,* CW 9ii, par. 30.
[75] Ibid.

The rest of this essay concerns issues that typically arise in the second half of life. Jung first speaks of the way consciousness develops, and then details some of the consequences. We've already touched on this—how at first we're tied to the world of the parents and then gradually get involved in the wider world:

> The ways that lead to conscious realization are many, but they follow definite laws. . . . The child begins its psychological life within very narrow limits, inside the magic circle of the mother and the family. With progressive maturation it widens its horizon and its own sphere of influence; its hopes and intentions are directed to extending the scope of personal power and possessions; desire reaches out to the world in ever-widening range; the will of the individual becomes more and more identical with the natural goals pursued by unconscious motivations. (par. 331a)

That's youth, the first half of life, and ain't it grand! There's nowhere to go but up. You start off with the world as your oyster. There's no end to oysters and over the years you open as many as you can.

What if you lose interest in oysters?

Well, that's what often happens at some point, and it's why Jung pinpoints the middle period of life as a time of great psychological importance. You've made your mark but so what? Is that all there is? What does it all mean? What comes next? Is there something else you'd rather do or be?

Is there life after oysters? . . .

Listen to these next few sentences with an ear to how they might apply to someone who built up a business from scratch, or a woman whose kids have grown up and left home:

> Thus man [and woman too] breathes his own life into things, until finally they begin to live of themselves and to multiply; and imperceptibly he is overgrown by them. Mothers are overtaken by their children, men by their own creations, and what was originally brought into being only with labour and the greatest effort can no

longer be held in check. First it was passion, then it became duty, and finally an intolerable burden, a vampire that battens on the life of its creator. (par. 331a)

I knew a man who started his own business when he was thirty-two years old. By the time he was fifty he had everything he'd ever dreamed of. He was respected and he could afford to do anything he wanted. At the pinnacle of his success, he gradually became aware that he was losing interest. Where he had passionately believed in what he was doing, now he began to doubt its value. Where he used to leap out of bed at dawn to greet the day, he started sleeping in till ten. Instead of promoting his products, pursuing new markets and so on—the kind of challenges he used to thrive on—he would chew a pencil and stare out the window, day-dreaming. He looked at what he had created and found he had no energy for it. He continued to run things because he was afraid that without him the business would fall apart, but he resented it.

When he came to me he was anxious and very depressed. "I have a wonderful life," he said, and burst into tears.

Of course he didn't have a wonderful life at all. What he did have was a wonderful persona. Now it had cracked. It took six months in analysis for him to realize that. He kept coming back to this question, it plagued him no end: "When you have everything you want, what else is there?"

Women? Fast cars?

Travel?

Peace and quiet!

Those may be your fantasies, but they weren't his. He was a home-body, a family man. He was comfortable with his wife and had no interest in other women. Foreign places didn't attract him at all. Fast cars? He drove an old Ford pick-up and he couldn't see himself in anything else.

"It's embarrassing," he said, "I lack for nothing and I'm not happy. Why not?"

What did you say?

Nothing. I know some theory and I've experienced my own process, that's all. His situation fit some patterns I'm familiar with, but he himself was unique. I trusted that his unconscious would come up with an answer. If you pay attention, it usually responds.

However, his question is one I often hear from someone of that age. As Jung says here:

> Middle life is the moment of greatest unfolding, when a man still gives himself to his work with his whole strength and his whole will. But in this very moment evening is born, and the second half of life begins. Passion now changes her face and is called duty; "I want" becomes the inexorable "I must," and the turnings of the pathway that once brought surprise and discovery become dulled by custom. (par. 331a)

That describes almost exactly the feeling this man had. Of course it happens to women as well as men. It doesn't seem to matter whether they've lived a traditional lifestyle, where they've been the homemaker and the man brought home the bacon, or if they've had an active career of their own. Gender isn't a factor in a midlife crisis, it's a general psychological issue.

At some point these people just run out of steam. They have dark thoughts and terrible moods. They don't have their former energy or ambition. Their outlook is bleak. In fact, they have all the symptoms of an acute neurosis.

Suicidal?

Sometimes, but not seriously, or else the messiness of doing it stops them . . . You understand, I'm talking about people who experience a crisis in the transition from one stage of life to another. That's quite natural, and where it *doesn't* happen, you have to wonder. I don't work with psychotics, I'm not trained to. I only see those who are neurotic, like you and me.

I don't think of myself as neurotic.

Who does? But neurosis isn't a dirty word. Jung described it simply as self-division, an inner state of disunity. "When you are not quite at one with yourself in a given matter," he says, "you are approaching a neurotic condition."[76] In terms of the Axiom of Maria, this is just the movement from one to two.[77] Once you were happy in the Garden, now you aren't. You have a conflict. You're caught between opposites and you don't know what to do.

It doesn't sound attractive.

As a matter of fact, Jung thought this was a particularly desirable development, not only on a personal level but also for the survival of mankind. He looked at the world scene—this was in the fifties, during the Cold War, with East and West in opposing camps—and saw a distinct possibility of nuclear war. He thought the only way it might be avoided was if enough people worked on their personal conflicts. Here's what he wrote:

> The psychological rule says that when an inner situation is not made conscious, it happens outside, as fate. That is to say, when the individual remains undivided and does not become conscious of his inner opposite, the world must perforce act out the conflict and be torn into opposing halves.[78]

On an individual level, once you realize you have a conflict, the stage is set for a resolution. That comes through the work on yourself. And then, if you keep at it, you might get to feel good about life—you're "at one" again. The difference is that now you're rather more conscious—you have a good idea of *why.* You know where you were, what you've been through, and you're not so scared of what might come next.

Of course, this doesn't happen overnight, and usually not on your own. You really need to have someone to say things to that you'd never dream of saying to anyone else—a professional, someone you

---

[76] "The Tavistock Lectures," *The Symbolic Life,* CW 18, par. 383.
[77] See above, p. 86.
[78] *Aion,* CW 9ii, par. 126.

trust and pay to listen. That's what analysis is all about, it's a joint effort between two people doing their best to understand what makes you tick.

Why not just talk it through with friends?

Because they're as unconscious as you are! All you get is sympathy and the projection of how they'd feel in your shoes. You can continue to feel sorry for yourself.

Analysis is pretty expensive.

Well, it's not cheap and it does involve a lot of time and energy. But nobody I've worked with was independently wealthy. It's a matter of priorities. You put your money—and money is a long-standing symbol of energy—into what you value. If you hurt enough, you find a way. You make sacrifices.

I thought it was just for an elite.

Elite? I'm not sure what you mean. Analysis is for people like you and me. Of course, it isn't suitable for everyone, and not everybody benefits from it. Analysis isn't a panacea, it's a process.

Do you think everyone needs it?

No, but when you're overwhelmed by conflicts or having difficulties in a relationship, or if you come to a point where you feel life has no meaning, you could do worse than go into analysis.

I'd like to be a better person.

Well, analysis isn't about improving yourself. Good, better, best, who's to say? Value judgments are not the concern in analysis. The most it can do is help you become conscious of who you are. You get to know your strengths and weaknesses. The goal isn't perfection, but completeness.

Of course, completeness is an ideal too, and it's no more reachable than perfection, but as Jung put it, "The goal is important only as an idea; the essential thing is the *opus* [that's the work on yourself] which leads to the goal: *that* is the goal of a lifetime."[79]

You see, what we're culturally inclined to stigmatize as a nervous breakdown may in fact be a person's salvation. It can be your wake-up call to a more satisfying way of life. Depression, for instance, that awful listless feeling when you don't know what to do, is often a sign that your psyche is prompting you to a new level of awareness. Never mind what once made you happy. The question is, what will do the trick *now?* Where does your energy want to go?

That could become a moral issue.

Yes, if your energy wants to go in a direction that's socially unacceptable or where you think it shouldn't. To your local bank vault, for instance, or your neighbor's wife . . .

Excuse me, what does neurosis have to do with relationship?

What doesn't it! Everything, if you think of neurosis—call it a nervous breakdown if you like—as a spur to consciousness. Neurosis is a needle in the unconsciously constructed haystack of life. If you get needled enough, maybe you'll be motivated to start individuating. In fact, Jung suggests that individuation is a task imposed on us by nature, and one way or another we'll be drawn into it:

> If [a man] does this [pursues the goal of wholeness] consciously and intentionally, he avoids all the unhappy consequences of repressed individuation. In other words, if he voluntarily takes the burden of completeness on himself, he need not find it "happening" to him against his will in a negative form. This is as much as to say that anyone who is destined to descend into a deep pit had better set about it with all the necessary precautions rather than risk falling into the hole backwards.[80]

And if you accept Jung's premise, that the possibility of having a psychological relationship depends on being conscious, then we're

---

[79] "The Psychology of the Transference," *The Practice of Psychotherapy,* CW 16, par. 400.
[80] *Aion,* CW 9ii, par. 125.

bound to consider what contributes to *becoming* conscious.

Or what gets in the way of it.

Yes. My own view is that neurosis is virtually a prerequisite for individuation. If you think of individuation as the conscious movement toward wholeness, you can't get started on the journey until you don't feel whole! Until then, you're just unconscious.

Jung ends paragraph 331a with these remarks about what is likely to happen at the midpoint of life:

> The wine has fermented and begins to settle and clear. Conservative tendencies develop if all goes well; instead of looking forward one looks backward, most of the time involuntarily, and one begins to take stock, to see how one's life has developed up to this point. The real motivations are sought and real discoveries are made. The critical survey of himself and his fate enables a man to recognize his peculiarities. But these insights do not come to him easily; they are gained only through the severest shocks.

You see, you can mope around forever with the vague feeling that life has lost its glow—feel sorry for yourself and blame others. It generally takes a shock of some kind to get you to acknowledge that *you* have to change. This can happen in all sorts of ways—an accident, illness, somebody close to you dies, or maybe you have yet another affair that doesn't work out . . .

What happened to your fifty-year-old entrepreneur?

Well, I have to say it was one of my most successful cases. He finally went bankrupt.

Successful?!

Yes. After a couple of years in analysis he realized where his energy wanted to go and he went with it. He said to hell with the business world, he wanted to make pots! He lost almost everything, but he turned his leaden life into gold. Of course those close to him didn't see it that way. His wife left, his children thought he was crazy. He could live with all that because he knew what he was doing.

But he lost his wife! Wasn't he interested in having a psychological relationship?

As a matter of fact, he was. But when it came to the crunch, *she* wasn't. His wife preferred the status quo. They had had a symbiotic relationship and gradually he got free of it. The more independent he became—the more he knew his own mind—the less power she had over him. That was a real shock to her! But it didn't motivate her to work on herself, she just found someone else.

The point here is that when you get a handle on what drives you, you no longer relate to other people in the same old way. For instance, you're no longer tied to someone by a complex, you're free to choose. Relating to this new you takes some adjustment.

I know what you mean. I'm a member of Alanon, the support group for friends and relatives of people in Alcoholics Anonymous. If you want to continue a relationship with a reformed alcoholic, you too have to be willing to change.

Yes, and the same is true for the friends and mates of those in analysis. Of course even then—if the partner sincerely wants to change, and does—there's no guarantee the relationship will survive. Quite as many relationships break up when one goes into analysis, as are cemented.

And if they're both in analysis?

The same thing. Each finds his or her own measure. I know those who have gone into analysis determined to become more loveable to their mate. After a time they realize they've projected a good deal of themselves onto the other person, and when the projections are taken back there's nothing, or not much, to hold them together.

That's sad.

I don't know. Maybe the sooner you realize it the better. In any case, the motivation that originally takes people into analysis generally takes a back seat to something completely unexpected, and this often manifests in the desire simply to live their own experiential truth and accept the consequences.

So what's the point in working on a relationship?

None at all, if you think it will get better by talking about it. To my mind, this puts the cart before the horse. Work on yourself and a good relationship will follow. You can either accept who you are and find a relationship that fits, or twist yourself out of shape and get what you deserve.

It's not easy to accept this brutal truth. I don't know that it's even possible before a certain age. As Jung points out toward the end of this essay, "Every period of life has its own psychological truth." (par. 343) The aims of the second half of life are different from those of the first. This may seem self-evident, but you can't really appreciate what it means until you've been there. When it begins to look like you won't live forever, your priorities change.

Next week will be our last session, so in the meantime I'd like you to read the rest of Jung's essay. We won't get through it all, but at least we can look closely at what he calls the problem of the contained and the container. I think you'll find it's an interesting contribution to what's involved in a psychological relationship.

Interlude

Arnold bounced in, looking ten years younger.

"There's something about living in the country," he said, kicking off his boots. "It stirs the blood." He shook the snow off his parka and poured himself a cup of coffee. "How's it going?"

I spread my hands. "Well, you know . . . "

"I've got a new project," said Arnold. "Wanna hear?"

I nodded. I can't resist Arnold. He lives in a way I never could. I call it chaotic. He calls it life. When we shared a house in Zürich we almost came to blows.[81] Now we have . . . well, a psychological relationship.

"I'm going to do a documentary about the puer," said Arnold. "I got the idea from a parable. Listen to this:

> "The trousers fit too tightly at the crotch," complained Wen Po.
> "I cannot ruin a work of art," replied the tailor. "We shall have to remove your testicles."
> "Couldn't we just take them in?"[82]

I knew about the puer, of course—from *puer aeternus,* Latin for eternal child. Psychologically it refers to a man whose emotional life is stuck at an adolescent level. But I didn't see the connection.

"Don't you get it?" said Arnold. "Tight trousers are a message to the puer! The aging process goes on whether you grow up or not. The chest fills out, stomach muscles relax, the hairline recedes. All those inflated ideals of youth, situated in the head, slowly drift lower and settle around the middle. That's how you get a midlife tire!"

After some hesitation, I nodded. What the hell, I'm almost bald and my pants are tight.

Arnold was so excited his hands shook. I got a rag and wiped up

---

[81] See *The Survival Papers,* pp. 99ff.

[82] David Berry, "Concession," in *Pocket Pool,* with photographs by Rolf Lockwood (Toronto: Peppermint Press, 1975).

the coffee spots.

"The typical puer," said Arnold, "romps gayly into middle age, with enough rewards to avoid becoming conscious of the obvious. But a pair of pants that no longer fits, well now, there's an undeniable sign of age. Even squash twice a week won't keep you trim. That's when fitness clubs and hair transplant mongers close in, inviting us to simulate youth."

"The parable," I said, "speaks specifically of a tight crotch."

"Yes," said Arnold, "and that's an interesting metaphor. It suggests that one's pants—and I take this to symbolize an aspect of the persona not far removed from shoes, one's standpoint in the world —will no longer contain the demands of manhood that press upon the puer. Of course, more than literal sexuality is involved. The testicles aren't only organs of physical procreation. Together with the penis they're preeminently a symbol of the creative masculine."

I was impressed. Arnold isn't given to making speeches.

He drained his cup. "The interesting thing about the parable is that it assumes only two possible solutions to Wen Po's dilemma: remove the testicles or trim them to fit the cloth. The first would mean abrogating your creative potential; the second would be to continue, maimed, within a lifestyle that's no longer appropriate. Now, isn't this typical of a conflict situation where two radical solutions are immediately apparent, but neither one is satisfactory?"

I was beginning to see.

"From a Jungian point of view," said Arnold, "there's a third possibility: *a different pair of pants!* That would be a new lifestyle. The crafty tailor—I see him as one of those tricky characters the hero meets in fairy tales, a guy like Mercurius in alchemy—probably has *piles* of pants in the back room, and surely some would accommodate a larger crotch!"

I smiled. "He'd keep them for himself and special customers."

Arnold winked. "And they'd be very, very expensive."

Seminar Five

I'd like to move directly to what Jung calls the problem of the contained and the container. Just about everything we've talked about in these sessions appears somewhere else in Jung's work. The marriage essay is the only place he presents this model of a relationship where one of the partners is contained by the other.

Yes?

I've been thinking about what we discussed last week. Why do some people have a midlife crisis—become neurotic—when others in more or less similar circumstances don't?

Well, nobody knows for sure. I think Jung's answer would be that the individual psyche knows both its limits and its potential. If your limits are being exceeded, or your potential isn't being realized, then some kind of breakdown can occur. The psyche itself acts to correct the situation.

But not always . . .

Maybe not everyone's up to it. Later in this essay Jung states his belief that psychological development is "a question of race, family, education, talent, and passion":

> Nature is aristocratic. The normal man is a fiction, although certain generally valid laws do exist. Psychic life is a development that can easily be arrested on the lowest levels. It is as though every individual had a specific gravity, in accordance with which he either rises, or sinks down, to the level where he reaches his limit. His views and convictions will be determined accordingly. (par. 343)

If it's any consolation, Jung thought neurosis was most likely to strike a "higher" type of person. He wrote:

> There are vast masses of the population who, despite their notorious unconsciousness, never get anywhere near a neurosis. The few who

are smitten by such a fate are really persons of the "higher" type who, for one reason or another, have remained too long on a primitive level. Their nature does not in the long run tolerate persistence in what is for them an unnatural torpor. As a result of their narrow conscious outlook and their cramped existence they save energy; bit by bit it accumulates in the unconscious and finally explodes in the form of a more or less acute neurosis.[83]

I'd go to the hospital if that happened. Doctors know what to do, they're trained.

Doctors are trained in what to do when you're physically sick. They look for the cause and then try to cure it. If there's nothing organically wrong, they're at a loss.

When I was depressed last year my doctor gave me tranquillizers. They helped a lot.

Pills can contain your mood and make you feel better, but they won't touch the real problem. You have to deal with that yourself.

The real problem?

The real problem is *you,* your psyche's out of whack. Depression, anxiety, confusion—and especially conflict—these are the common symptoms of neurosis. Sure, something's causing them, but they generally have a purpose too. You'll never find out what that is if you just treat the symptoms.

   In analysis, you know, we pay hardly any attention to symptoms, they're just the tip of the iceberg. We look at what's floating around below the surface and try to bring that to light. As Jung says, "Only what is really oneself has the power to heal."[84]

Psychiatrists?

If you're lucky, you might find one who's had some personal analy-

---

[83] "The Function of the Unconscious," *Two Essays on Analytical Psychology,* CW 7, par. 291.
[84] "The Relations between the Ego and the Unconscious," ibid., par. 258.

sis or therapy and who'll listen. Otherwise they're tied to the medical model. Their standard tools are pills, strait jackets and padded cells.

My cousin had shock treatment. It made him wobbly.

When all else fails, fry the brain!

Actually, I wouldn't be too quick to judge. Jung himself was ambivalent. In 1957, just a few years before he died, he conceded that some mental problems might be organic as well as, or even instead of, psychological.[85] My observations here have to do only with your common and garden variety neurosis, not extreme disorders like schizophrenia or some other psychosis.

You see, the normally healthy psyche is a self-regulating system. Jung believed—and it's my experience too—that there's a natural and ongoing process within the psyche that aims to maintain or re-establish a balance between consciousness and the unconscious.

That's what he called compensation.

Yes. Usually it's invisible. It only becomes noticeable when we come up against some situation in the outside world—or maybe in ourselves—that we have difficulty adapting to. Then we get these so-called neurotic symptoms.

More than fifty years ago Jung was grilled on this by a group of doctors in London. They were baffled by what he was telling them. Here's a sample of their exchange:

> *Question:* "I think we can assume then, Professor Jung, that you regard the outbreak of a neurosis as an attempt at self-cure, as an attempt at compensation . . . ?"
>
> *Jung:* "Absolutely."
>
> *Question:* "I understand, then, that the outbreak of a neurotic illness, from the point of view of a man's development, is something favorable?"

---

[85] See "Recent Thoughts on Schizophrenia," *The Psychogenesis of Mental Disease,* CW 3.

Jung: "That is so, and I am glad you bring up that idea. That is really my point of view. . . . In many cases we have to say: 'Thank heaven he could make up his mind to be neurotic.' Neurosis is really an attempt at self-cure, just as any physical illness is partly an attempt at self-cure. . . . It is an attempt of the self-regulating psychic system to restore the balance, in no way different from the function of dreams—only rather more forceful and drastic."[86]

I was on my knees when I first read this, and I was greatly cheered. What a relief, I wasn't necessarily crazy! Of course, if Jung was right it also meant I couldn't expect someone else to fix me up, to make it all better. I had to accept some personal responsibility for what was happening. But that's another story.[87]

You were neurotic?

Was I neurotic?!

But you're an analyst!

I am now. I wouldn't be an analyst if I hadn't fallen apart. Do you think it's a profession you choose?

I'd like to be one.

I'd be glad to discuss it with you later.

In paragraph 331c Jung works up to his views on container and contained by pointing out that in any relationship there are invariably differences in the degree of spiritual development of the partners.

I imagine we all have our own idea of what this word "spiritual" means. Jung himself used it in a number of different ways, so let's be clear what he means by it here. In his own words,

> I do not wish to imply an especially rich or magnanimous nature. Such is not the case at all. I mean, rather, a certain complexity of mind or nature, comparable to a gem with many facets as opposed to the simple cube. (par. 331c)

---

86 "The Tavistock Lectures," *The Symbolic Life,* CW 18, pars. 382ff.
87 See *The Survival Papers.*

To my mind, this just means that the needs and aspirations of one partner are simpler and more easily satisfied than are those of the other. The first Jung calls the contained, and the second, the more complicated nature, the container.

I know some complicated people—you never know what's going on, what they're thinking or feeling or anything.

Jung goes on to say that the more complicated nature may have a tendency to dissociation—Jung says they "have the capacity to split off irreconcilable traits of character for considerable periods"—and so appear to be simpler than he or she actually is. Such a person has "a peculiar charm." This is as much as to say that your pig in a poke may turn out to be a weasel. I think we've already been alerted to that possibility in our discussion of the shadow. You can fall in love with a persona but what you get is the whole hog.

The more important point Jung makes is that the simpler personality can be absorbed, as it were—Jung says "swamped"—by the "labyrinthine nature" of the other and utterly consumed in keeping track of it.

What do you think that would that look like?

A traditional marriage? The man goes to work in the morning and returns at night to tell his wife what happened.

She'd be content to live through him.

That's one possibility, and Jung touches on it when he says:

> It is almost a regular occurrence for a woman to be wholly contained, spiritually, in her husband, and for a husband to be wholly contained, emotionally, in his wife. (par. 331c)

In such a situation the man would be active in the outside world, using his thinking function—whether he's good at it or not!—and only thanks to his wife would he come to see how he felt about it all. He'd mediate to her what was happening in business and politics and so on, and she'd help him understand what was going on in himself. In terms of our discussion last week of the archetypal masculine and feminine, his energies would be focused on Logos activities and hers on those areas having to do with Eros.

Couldn't it be the other way round?

Of course. The dominance of the contrasexual complexes, anima and animus, can change the picture entirely. And nowadays the woman is just as likely to be the breadwinner as the man.

Wouldn't their typology also be a factor?

Yes.

The traditional way was the norm in Jung's day.

Yes, and it still applies to many relationships. The social scene is dramatically different, but has the psychological reality shifted so much? Look around you. Who remembers birthdays and sends out the Christmas cards? Who tells who how to vote? Who's in charge of the couple's savings, what to invest in? Who manages their social life? As I pointed out last week, the psyche is conservative. *Plus ça change, plus que la même chose,* as the French would say.

Plus . . .?

Women still look to their man for what to think, and men depend on their woman for what to feel.

Not in my family.

Well, I'm sure we can all think of exceptions, but this is not something we need to argue about, it isn't important in the context. I think Jung's point here is simply that each partner in a relationship may be contained by the other, only in different ways—one emotionally, the other spiritually. Naturally this leaves the other, man or woman, in the role of container.

What about a same-sex relationship?

There's no theoretical difference. Who's container and who's contained depends on the individual psychology of the partners.

In paragraph 332 Jung describes the situation from the standpoint of the contained:

> The one who is contained feels himself to be living entirely within the confines of his marriage; his attitude to the marriage partner is undivided; outside the marriage there exist no essential obligations and no binding interests.

It isn't really clear whether Jung intends these remarks to apply to the one who feels contained emotionally or contained spiritually.

I've puzzled over that myself. But I think what Jung says holds true in either case. One way or another, emotionally or spiritually, one partner feels contained by the other. The one who feels contained is focused entirely on the relationship—"undivided," says Jung—and happy within it, more or less

That's me. I can't imagine not being married. It's nice and cozy.

Well, so far so good. But there's a shadow side to that, like there is to everything—the possibility of discontent. It lies not in a search outside the relationship for someone or something else, but in what Jung goes on to describe as the contained person's "disquieting dependence" on the container:

> The unpleasant side of this otherwise ideal partnership is the disquieting dependence upon a personality that can never be seen in its entirety, and is therefore not altogether credible or dependable.

What would that feel like?

Insecurity?

I think so, there'd be a nagging suspicion that what feels so good can't last. As we shall see, this is not what's going on in the container-partner.

Being the container feels powerful, full of possibilities. Some are potentially upsetting to the status quo, others are merely exciting. But that's all below the surface and doesn't normally get in the way of a relationship, at least not at the beginning. The container is genuinely looking for, and expects to find, his or her mirror image in the other. It's not a question of deception but unconsciousness. The juices are there, you go with them.

Notice here that we're talking about the search for personal completion, the projection of one's other half—in the Platonic sense we talked about last time[88]—onto one's partner. Jung's premise is that the more complicated nature, the container, has an unconscious drive to be undivided in union with the other, while the contained one feels he or she has already found it.

That would be togetherness . . .

Yes, "one heart and one soul." It's the typical picture during courtship and it can even last through the honeymoon.

Unfortunately, as time goes on it becomes clear that life is not what we want it to be. We're mere pawns in a psychological chess game. It turns out that the contained one is not the match the container was looking for at all—he or she is *really* quite simple and uncomplicated—and the one who initially felt contained is in bed with a problematic container . . .

What might happen then?

The contained one would feel confused and bewildered.

Bereft!

And that's not the half of it. Jung puts it like this:

> While [the container] is seeking in [the contained] all the subtleties and complexities that would complement and correspond to his own facets, he is disturbing the other's simplicity. Since in normal circumstances simplicity always has the advantage over complexity, he will very soon be obliged to abandon his efforts to arouse subtle and intricate reactions in a simpler nature.

He'd stop trying and just withdraw.

Possibly. Jung goes on:

---

[88] See above, p. 87.

The simpler nature works on the more complicated like a room that is too small, that does not allow him enough space. The complicated nature, on the other hand, gives the simpler one too many rooms with too much space, so that she never knows where she really belongs. So it comes about quite naturally that the more complicated contains the simpler. (par. 333)

It sounds here like the man is bound to be the container.

It does, but in the original German the terms aren't attached to a particular gender. (par. 333, note 2) The situation could just as easily be reversed, I know many cases where it was. In any event, container and contained are not states of being that are immutable. This is a model of what's possible in a relationship. Like typology, it's a useful tool to figure out where you are.

So it's a changing situation?

Yes. You can feel contained one day, dependent, and quite in charge the next. Or as container, you breeze through the day, confident, nothing can go wrong. The next day you can barely haul yourself out of bed, you're frazzled and long to feel contained. That's the see-saw of being human. And in a psychological relationship—where by definition the partners are conscious of what's going on—allowance is automatically, and graciously, made for the opposite.

Now, this remark by Jung that the container can feel like he or she is living in too small a room. What might that look like?

Restlessness? . . .

Frustration.

Sometimes I wait up all night and she doesn't come home. I read and watch tv and all the time I feel these worms in my gut. Where is she? What's she up to?

Where does that leave you?

Ummm . . . I don't know. She says she loves me, but I have no idea what I'm worth to her.

Your self-worth depends on her?

Well . . . I have no one else.

It leaves you in a vacuum, that's where. Women have all the cards.

You can bet your heart out, you'll never win.

What I see is men have it made. Women aren't the power behind the throne, that's just a sop. We get a few licks in, that's all.

You wish!

Wait, wait. You're complexed and you're fighting paper tigers. In the battle of the sexes, it's not a matter of winning or losing. It's just plain dumb to think that way. The real question is, can you hold your own? It's a plain and simple psychological issue. Do you know who you are? Do you know what's happening and why?

Man or woman, you don't need to be a pawn. There are knights and bishops in this world, and rooks and queens, and then the king, of course. You can be any one of these, it's up to you. Why there's no limit to what you can become. On the great psychological chess board of life there's a square for you! . . .

Sorry, I was carried away.

Let's take a break.

*

We were talking about the container, the more complicated one, feeling constricted by the simpler nature, like living in a room that's too small, while the contained one is left to rattle around in too many rooms with too much space.

Thinking dark thoughts.

Crying in the night.

Yes, and the tension builds. The container paces his—pardon me, or her—cell. The contained one sees the relationship slipping away and tries to hold on. This has the opposite of the desired effect. In the middle of paragraph 333, Jung says:

> The more the contained clings, the more the container feels shut out of the relationship. The contained pushes into it by her clinging, and the more she pushes, the less the container is able to respond. He therefore tends to spy out of the window, no doubt unconsciously at first; but with the onset of middle age there awakens in him a more insistent longing for that unity and undividedness which is especially necessary to him on account of his dissociated nature. At this juncture things are apt to occur that bring the conflict to a head. He becomes conscious of the fact that he is seeking completion, seeking the contentedness and undividedness that have always been lacking.

I've been married more than once. My first wife was entirely too dependent, she couldn't make a shopping list on her own.

I don't know, maybe all she wanted was some company.

I think this passage is an explanation for extramarital affairs.

Yes, it's one of the things that's "apt to occur."

Maybe he'd run into one of those marriage wreckers . . .[89]

Well, better to brave the fire than eat your heart out watching tv, don't you think?

Not if you're married. I couldn't condone that.

Anyway, the container's defection may not involve a third person. It may simply manifest in withdrawal or disinterest—disaffection of some kind.

My wife's lover is the local library.

Whether he—or she—goes out looking for what's missing at home, or just makes do with a fantasy life, it's a chimera.

Chimer . . . ?

An illusion.

---

[89] See above, pp. 72-73.

Will you stop doing that?! You sound just like my father.

Illusion, house of mirrors, all that. You see, what the container is really looking for is someone to be contained by. That's the unconscious shadow side. And conversely, the contained one wants someone to contain . . .

Let's say the container does have an affair, what then?

Well, it would be a shock to the contained one, that's for sure, though no more than was unconsciously feared and half-expected. As Jung says:

> For the contained this is only a confirmation of the insecurity she has always felt so painfully; she discovers that in the rooms which apparently belonged to her there dwell other, unwished-for guests.

It felt to me like the whole house had been invaded.

It's quite a poignant metaphor, isn't it?—*"In the rooms which apparently belonged to her there dwell other, unwished-for guests."*

Of course, "apparently" is the operative word here. The rooms didn't belong to her—or him—at all. At best, they were rented. But as we know, intimate relationships tend to breed a sense of ownership. The loved one is your territory.

It's a patriarchal attitude, droit de seigneur *and all that . . .*

Until not so long ago a man could even get away with killing his wife's lover. He was thought to have a perfect right to defend his property, it was part of his honor.

If a woman did the same, she'd be stoned or burned at the stake.

Men get away with murder.

Yes, that's the way it goes. Those who have the power use it.

But the fact is, women are just as prone to the feeling of ownership as men. It's the basis for jealousy on both sides, and it's behind the sense of betrayal when we suspect our pillow-talk has been shared with someone else.

That's natural, isn't it? It's instinctive.

I suppose so.

Animals fight tooth and nail for what's theirs.

If God had been satisfied with what's natural we'd still be swinging from trees.

Maybe we can agree that denying the instincts is not the answer. As Jung points out here later, the turn of events that interrupts the first-half-of-life harmony between container and contained is a necessary development—psychologically, that is—and "any attempt to create a spiritual attitude by splitting off and suppressing the instincts is a falsification." (par. 336)

You may recall Jung's pithy statement:

> Too much of the animal distorts the civilized man, too much civilization makes sick animals.[90]

To me, in this context, it would mean the container should not deny the attraction to someone else—if indeed that's what happens— and the contained one can't just swallow the hurt. The question is, can our instinctive reactions be modified, or even transformed, by consciousness? Can we change the course of our lives by becoming aware of what's going on?

At the end of paragraph 333 Jung suggests the possible effect on the contained one:

> The hope of security vanishes, and this disappointment drives her in on herself, unless by desperate and violent efforts she can succeed in forcing her partner to capitulate, and in extorting a confession that his longing for unity was nothing but a childish or morbid fantasy.

I've been through that, it's a mug's game.

You lose your self-respect, begging for affection.

Jung goes on—and may I remind you, the text reads "she" and "her"

---

[90] See above, note 12.

but it applies just as well to a man:

> If these tactics do not succeed, her acceptance of failure may do her a
> real good, by forcing her to recognize that the security she was so
> desperately seeking in the other is to be found in herself. In this way
> she finds herself and discovers in her own simpler nature all those
> complexities which the container had sought for in vain.

Do you see what this means?

*She comes to know those sides of herself she'd projected onto the
container-partner . . .*

Yes, just when she thought she'd lost it all, she suddenly finds a
treasure! . . . Isn't that ironic?

Meanwhile, the container, whom one might think is footloose and
fancy free, gleefully exploring a spacious new apartment, is hard
pressed not to fall apart!—

> If the container does not break down in face of what we are wont to
> call "unfaithfulness," but goes on believing in the inner justification
> of his longing for unity, he will have to put up with his self-divi-
> sion for the time being. (par. 334)

Self-division, meaning internal conflict?

Yes. You see, the container may have found a new soul-mate . . .

The match he's been longing for . . .

. . . but he still feels something for the original partner. So he's torn
apart. There's a splitting of the personality. As you may recall, this
means the complexes get activated.

In the container?

In both.

All hell breaks loose.

Yes, if you haven't been there you can imagine what it looks like.
Typically, on one side—from the one who hoped to be contained—
there are tearful accusations and cries of "poor me," the abandoned

child syndrome. On the other, there's slinking around, indecision and a pervasive feeling of guilt. On both sides there are anxious days and sleepless nights.

They're both dissociated?

Yes, there's no ego, both have been thrown into the unconscious. The situation is a pressure cooker, full of affect. It could blow at any time. Steaming with complexes, people collapse, they have heart attacks and strokes. When the lid goes, they kick their kids, they abuse each other and sometimes they kill. It's not a pretty sight and nobody feels good. It's a huge personal and social problem nowadays.

Excuse me, I thought this was supposed to be positive.

Well, potentially it is—it can lead to an increase in consciousness.

You see, the disintegration of the personality isn't an ominous event if you understand it as an opportunity for new life. Remember what Jung said about neurosis?—"It is an attempt of the self-regulating psychic system to restore the balance."[91]

In an unconscious relationship there's a joint psyche, so to speak. Container and contained is only one way to describe it. Primitive identity is another. It works, up to a point, then you're on your own. At some point you have to grow up and provide for yourself. Otherwise the relationship becomes mechanical, you just go through the motions. Mom and Pop, collective.

Why doesn't it go on working?

I don't know. Jung's view is that we're meant to realize in ourselves what we instinctively look for outside. And if we don't, if we settle for less, the unconscious rears up and consciousness breaks down.

I think that's the gist of the next paragraph here:

This is what happens very frequently about the midday of life, and in this wise our miraculous human nature enforces the transition that leads from the first half of life to the second. It is a metamorphosis

---

[91] See above, p. 107.

from a state in which man is only a tool of instinctive nature, to another in which he is no longer a tool, but himself: a transformation of nature into culture, of instinct into spirit. (par. 335)

Looking outside for your other half, your soul-mate, may be instinctive, but in the long run, in the psychic economy of the individual, it's not acceptable. And right here is Jung's particular contribution to an understanding of what's involved in a psychological relationship. What from a conventional point of view seems like disaster may in fact be a gift from the gods. He says:

A dissociation is not healed by being split off, but by more complete disintegration. All the powers that strive for unity, all healthy desire for selfhood, will resist the disintegration, and in this way he will become conscious of the possibility of an inner integration, which before he had always sought outside himself. He will then find his reward in an undivided self. (par. 334)

What do you make of that?

I don't understand it.

Both would be having a midlife crisis?

If they're lucky! And that's what often transforms an unconscious, instinctive relationship into a conscious one. Container and contained are opposites, you see. The conflict between them can be a powerful spur to consciousness.

Between the partners?

Yes, but also, and more important I think, within oneself.

What I have in mind here is Jung's belief that the potential resolution of any conflict is constellated by consciously holding the tension between the opposites. Jung called it the transcendent function.[92] It's not a whole lot different from the traditional Christian idea of grace—"the peace that transcendeth understanding"—except that it doesn't come from a God out there, it wells up inside. In one of his last works Jung describes what happens like this:

---

[92] See *The Structure and Dynamics of the Psyche,* CW 8, pars. 131ff.

[A conflict] requires a real solution and necessitates a third thing in which the opposites can unite. Here the logic of the intellect usually fails, for in a logical antithesis there is no third. The "solvent" can only be of an irrational nature. In nature the resolution of opposites is always an energic process: she acts *symbolically* in the truest sense of the word, doing something that expresses both sides, just as a waterfall visibly mediates between above and below.[93]

Now, what do you think a satisfactory resolution between container and contained might look like? Anyone?

They'd agree to differ?

They'd go their own way.

I think they'd have to acknowledge their separateness and put some distance between them, at least psychologically. Maybe in the long run they would actually part, but they shouldn't do that just to put an end to the conflict.

It's what people usually do.

Yes, but that's no resolution at all. It's just giving up, throwing in the towel. They find themselves back on what's been called the same old marriage-go-round. They get rid of one partner for another, that's easy enough, but there's no increase in consciousness and the internal split isn't healed. Unless the tension is held, nothing changes psychologically. You're right back at square one.

If you can stand the tension—wait and do nothing—you stand a chance of experiencing what Jung called the transcendent function. What this looks like in the outside world is different in every case, but psychologically it manifests in *self-containment.* That's the most satisfactory resolution, the reward, the light at the end of the neurosis-tunnel. It's what I think is involved in what Jung calls "a transformation of nature into culture, of instinct into spirit." (par. 335)

When you're self-contained, you see, you don't look to another person for completion. You don't identify with others and you're not

---

93 "The Conjunction," *Mysterium Coniunctionis,* CW 14, par. 705.

victimized by projection. You know where you stand and you live by your personal truth—come what may. You have what Jung calls here an undivided self. In the classical Axiom of Maria, it's "the One as the fourth."[94]

You don't need anyone else?

That's right. Well, at least compared to before. Nobody's completely one, we've talked about that. And we're never completely conscious, we've talked about that too. Projection and conflict are always possible. That's no bad thing, they keep us on our toes. Maybe next time we'll be more conscious.

Think of the difference between being in love and loving. When you're in love, you absolutely *need* the other person, you can't live without him—or her. That's okay to start off with, who can help it? It's only natural, in the sense Jung uses the term when he says, "It is the natural and given thing for unconscious contents to be projected"[95]—but if it goes on like that, you kill the relationship. Need is not compatible with love. Need becomes the rationale for power over the other person, it leads to the contained one's fear of loss and the container's resentment.

When you're self-contained you're free of all that. You have your own sacred space, your own temenos. You might invite someone in, but you're not driven to. And you also respect the other's freedom and privacy. There's an optimum distance in every relationship. It evolves through trial and error and good will—if you stop pushing for more than you get.

My husband should hear this.

It sounds so lonely, all those rooms to yourself.

Actually, it's rather crowded. Get to know your complexes and you'll never be lonely again.

---

[94] See above, p. 86.

[95] "General Aspects of Dream Psychology," *The Structure and Dynamics of the Psyche,* CW 8, par. 507.

John Donne said no man is an island.

I like Donne, but maybe he was an extravert. Extraverts are far more comfortable relating to the outside world than to themselves.

They have introverted shadows, though.

Yes, and that's a good point. The unity or wholeness that container and contained look for in an intimate connection with someone else is only to be found within, in a relationship with *oneself.*

This involves getting to know your other sides, particularly your shadow and your contrasexual opposite, the anima or animus. It's not "natural," it's a very sophisticated development in the evolution of human consciousness. I dare say it's more important than putting a man on the moon. Jung seems to feel that not everyone can pull it off, but he believes it to be "the very essence of the psychological marriage relationship." (par. 337)

Well, we're almost out of time, but you see what a rich paradigm this is, container and contained.

Are there other ways to interpret it?

Maybe as many as there are analysts! In *Transformation of the God-Image,* Edinger sees it as a model of the relationship between the ego and the Self.

How would that work?

Well, the immensity of the Self—Jung said the Self might just as well be called the God within[96]—and the incalculable potentialities it represents would function as the container. The ego, earth-bound to the merely possible, would be the contained.

In the beginning of the developmental process, when we're young, there's an identity between ego and Self, just like that between lovers. And in the process of individuation, differentiating the

---

[96] "The Mana-Personality," *Two Essays on Analytical Psychology,* CW 7, par. 399.

ego from the Self can be just as painful as a separation between marriage partners. Edinger writes:

> One has to go through experiences of divorces and alienations and losses of connection to the God-image in order for the ego's relation to the Self to finally evolve into something conscious rather than something unconscious.[97]

You see, the world of the Self trickles down—or up—to the ego as consciousness realizes, or incarnates, certain aspects of the Self. This is a restriction for the Self and the possibilities it represents, like the container feeling cooped up in too small a room.

That's pretty deep.

It's all part of individuating, where a major task for ego-consciousness is to establish a psychological relationship with that "higher power" within. As you say, it's deep, but it parallels what's involved on a more mundane level between oneself and others.

One last question?

Is there a difference between a psychological relationship and the psychology of relationship?

Strictly speaking, a psychological relationship is one that's conscious, and the psychology of relationship is about what's involved in *becoming* conscious. Personally I think the difference is semantic, they're both about getting to know yourself.

Thank you for an interesting time.

---

[97] *Transformation of the God-Image,* p. 58.

Epilogue

Rachel laid the pages down and sighed.

Relief? Boredom? Something she ate? I can't always tell.

"It works," she said.

They were magic words to me. I leaped up and got my special elephant out of the safe. Rachel gave it to me when I turned fifty. It's solid silver and tarnishes in the air. I took it out of its silk wrapper and whispered in its ear.

"There's just one thing," said Rachel. "I did miss your own gut-level experience. You have a lot more to say, and not just from your head, about this topic. Especially the nitty-gritty—what goes on in a relationship between sexually intimate adults. Did something make you avoid it? Or wasn't that your goal? And if it was, why do I sense this *thing* sitting there, smiling, stiff and cocky, saying, "You can't leave me out!"

I looked up.

"It's all there, *sotto voce.*"

"Sotto . . . ?"

"Speak softly with your stick out of sight. If I were more explicit about what you and I know to be true, we'd have to mail it in a plain brown wrapper. That's not the business we're in. Before you know it, the vice squad would be at the door. I'd go to jail and have to wait 116 years for parole. You'd be a grass widow. Our little ones would go hungry."

"Never mind," said Rachel, slipping into something more comfortable. "Some day you'll find a way to say it straight. Intimacy with distance, that's the key."

I loosened my tie and bundled up my elephant.

"Yes," I said, "Maybe next time."

Index